The Torrington & T.H.S.
Facebook Posts
& a few other miscellaneous Facebook writings

by Paul Bentley

Cover design by Paul Bentley. Photo is the laying of the 1914 cornerstone at the "new" T.H.S. on Church Street. More information about this photo on p.70.

ISBN- 9781700512628

About The Author

Paul Bentley is a freelance writer and the author of the sort-of memoir *Sh*t A Teacher Thinks (and sometimes says)*, the novels *All Blood Runs Red* and *August Descending,* and seven other compilations of essays and feature pieces: *My Torrington Days: A Collection Of Writings, More Torrington Days (Volumes 1&2), Torrington Days Forever, Ye Olde Torrington Days, Those Glorious Torrington Days,* and *The Twilight Of Torrington Days*. All are available on Amazon. He lives in the Northeast with his wife and the great cat Ivy.

To all my Facebook friends and especially to the members of the "Torrington High School, Class Of 1966 & Friends" Facebook page. Through your cyber input, you've made this book possible.

Table Of Contents

1. Forward - p.1
2. Charlie Duggan Remembered - p.2
3. Laurence Square - p.5
4. The 1964 THS Band & Mr. Wheeler - p.6
4. 1960, the Iolanthe Production and Ethel Johnson - p.8
5. Herbie Lehmann - p.11
6. Addo and Ezio Bonetti - p.12
7. Nellie Sullivan - p.14
8. Abernethy's Store - p.18
9. Roland "Rollie" Spino - p.20
10. Teacher Appreciation - p.22
11. Teen Memories - p.24
12. Luis Thuillard and His 53-year-old Record - p.26
13. Helen Woodford - p.28
14. The Antique Car Caravan or Best To Stay In Torrington - p.30
15. They Died While In The Service - p.32
16. Warner Theatre Memories - p.34
17. T.H.S. Graduation Memories - p.38
18. Chet Torsiello - p.44
19. Delivering The Newspaper - p.46
20. Learning To Swim At The Torrington YMCA - p.50
21. The Hendey Machine Company - p.54
22. Rosie The Riveter, i.e. Torrington's Female Factory Workers - p. 60
23. Slow Down! Danger On Our City Streets - p.66
24. Catherine Clarissa Calhoun: An Accomplished Woman - p.68
25. Dorothea Cramer and Catherine Calhoun: Twin Lives - p.74
26. A Strange Question: Are you Jewish? - p.78
27. The Torrington Jewish Houses Of Worship - p.80
28. Bill Goring, Torrington's Premier Book Dealer - p.86
29. Torrington's Bookstores, 1885-1962 - p.92
30. Torrington's Bookstores, 1963-2019 - p. 97
31. Dinner On the Warner Stage - p.106

Table Of Contents
(continued)

32. Grocery Shopping In Torrington, or Am I Losing My Mind? - p. 108
33. A Celebrity Visits The Thrift Shop - p.112
34. Torrington Barbers and Barber Shops - p.114
35. Yankee Pedlar Memories - p.132
36. Lunch At The Yankee Pedlar On May 13, 1943 - p.136
37. Patricia McGowan Wald, Torrington's Top Legal Eagle - p.146
38. The Day T.H.S. Burned To The Ground - p.148
39. The Class Of 1913 and The T.H.S. Fire - p.150
40. Up In Flames: The TFD and Torrington Fires - p.154
41. The Camp Workcoeman Model - p.176
42. Seymour Franklin : Teacher, Coach, Good Guy - p.180
43. John Denza: Teacher, Administrator, Good Guy - p.182
44. Southeast School: The Walls Come A-Tumbling Down - p.184
45. Sledding In Torrington - p.186
46. Torrington Circuses, Under The Big Top - p.190
47. Strike Up The Corps, A 1929 Musical Weekend - p.196
48. Driver's Eduction, Proceed With Caution - p.202
49. The Cavallari Post - p.208
50. The Soap Box Derby: When Gravity Rules - p.212
51. THE Pond - p.228
52. The Genesis Of The T.H.S. "Red Raiders" - p.232
53. Autumn Thoughts At Hillside Cemetery - p.236
54. Epilogue - p.238

Forward

June 18, 2019. It recently occurred to me, that formal book writing aside, I do an awful lot of writing on Facebook. Between posting nearly daily on my own timeline and posting on the group page (Torrington High School, Class Of 1966 & Friends) which I created in December 2014, substantial effort goes into creating original posts and then responding to the myriad of feedback that's given.

The posts which I've included in this volume are only a small fraction of the total number of original entries and replies that I've both given and received in the last 11 years since I joined the social media site. They're in random chronological order, with the subject matter randomly mixed. Because this book is a retrospective look back on approximately 5 years of posts (since the founding of the THS page), it would have been very difficult, if not impossible, to obtain permission in hindsight from the plethora of individuals involved. Some of these quotes are from people I no longer have contact with; others are from people who have since died. Therefore, the response quotes are cited anonymously.

As always, it is my intent to insult no one, but rather to capture in these pages a sliver of a bygone Torrington that the mainly 1950 and 1960's generations experienced and loved.

It is my sincere hope that all readers of this book find something, hopefully *many* things, that recapture a happy time, person, or event.

Happy memory hunting.

(Right, the author at the old Barella's Tavern on Washington Avenue, May 2013.)

Post: Charlie Duggan Remembered

Who can ever forget Charlie Duggan? I remember Charlie calling me down to his office and telling me that if we didn't ease up on our homeroom teacher, Sue Hamill Pagano, he'd _____. It was a pretty damn good threat. . . Charlie could be a hot-cold guy and was VERY set in his ways. I don't think he ever quite accepted long hair and the counter-culture of the sixties, segueing to the disco seventies. Because I coached, and because our wives worked together at Torringford School, we saw each other quite a bit through a 20+ year period. I can't say we were ever friends, though he was a friendly guy to share a couple of drinks with. He liked scotch, but would stop cold after 3 drinks, or there about. Excellent control.

Responses included: "Being sent to his office was a memory that my mind can't erase." . . . (Below, students in 1966 lined up outside Charlie Duggan's Office.) . . . "I spent half of my senior year having

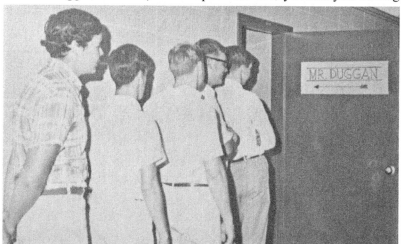

lunch with Mr. D in his office after a cafeteria incident. We actually became friends! I saw a few incidents that he had to deal with and heard the students' excuses. Upon leaving Tuna's (Duggan's nickname) office, I'd sometimes get a look from him and he'd start laughing. He'd say, 'See what I have to deal with?' - 'Yes Mr. Duggan!' " . . . "I went to his office and said I was sick and had to leave school. He said, 'Yes, and when can I expect Joan (my best friend)?' " . . . "Funny story regarding Duggan. Freshman year our homeroom teacher, Mr. Van Horn, had his nerdy hat disappear from the shelf where he kept it. The administration hauled me, Bill Celadon, and Vinnie Cavagnero down to the principal's office after school and grilled each of us separately, saying things like, 'Bill said you stole the hat, so you better just fess up.' None of us knew anything about the hat, and fortunately didn't crack. Duggan was my interrogator. (Right, Charlie Duggan in his office, 1969) What a zeke. I thought Duggan was a bully and a total asshole. There ya go." . . . "As far as Duggan being an a-hole goes, there's a lot of agreement, I

believe, on that point. I myself was sort of neutral about him." . . . "Charlie Duggan did have a bit of the bully in him. A mixed bag, and part of the mix was bully. I had a funny relationship with him. Very close when I was from 10-to-17-years-old. Then things went spittle south at West Hill Aquatic Camp where I worked with him. He treated me way better until the 1960s started to change everything, when student demonstration time and the early wars over hair (length) were obvious indicators of one's membership in the Communist Party. They sort of strained relations. Polarization. I saw him once again in 1974 at a THS football game. Very brief hello and goodbye. I asked after him with Maria Cravanzola once, but she said he just up and left Torrington and moved to the Cape. Mostly good memories though. RIP Charley Duggan." . . . "It cannot be said that nothing can be learned in detention. Mr. Duggan once taught me a coin trick while I was doing time." . . . "I remember him well - he was my history teacher. Great guy!" . . . "I remember him as Coach Duggan. I recall his wife as a teacher, elementary, I think." . . . "He was quite a man." . . . "He was a thug." . . . "I wouldn't call him a thug, though he wasn't peaches-and-cream either. Like all of us, he wasn't a simple person, but I hesitate to go beyond that since I'm very far from perfect myself." . . . "He tried to be formidable and intimidating. Was it an act, perhaps to make his job as discipline officer easier and more effective? Probably not, at least not totally. At THS it didn't help that in the later years of his career the teachers retreated into their rooms, and Charlie was pretty much the sole cop-on-the-beat." . . . "I loved Mr. Duggan - what a great guy!" . . . "He WAS intimidating, but a good man at heart. He had a sense-of-humor too. After the dress code was loosened in 1969, we both happened to be using urinals. He looked over at me and said, 'How ya doing, Abe?' (I had grown a beard). I did spend occasional time in detention, one time for getting into a fistfight in the cafeteria of all things!" . . .

(Left, Charlie Duggan as a social studies teacher in 1962)

Post: Laurence Square

A few weeks ago someone asked how Laurence Square in the North End got its name. I had the information then, just lazy about looking it up. OK, here goes with a quote from a long ago newspaper article: "In 1929 Laurence Park, a beautiful green with trees and benches, stretched in front of the North End shops between each side of Main Street. The land for the park was sold to the city for $1 in 1903 by A.P. Hine. Hine was superintendent of Coe Brass Company. . . Hine was a prosperous land owner. Later in 1908, the green was named Laurence Park in memory of his son Laurence who died suddenly in 1902. Young Hine was a student at Hotchkiss school where he sustained a shoulder injury while playing football. During one of many subsequent trips to a Manhattan hospital to receive medical attention, he was enjoying his evening meal in an adjoining hotel building when dynamite exploded from a subway construction site below. The explosion injured and killed several people in the hotel including young Hine. . The green was removed in 1932 and replaced by a large traffic circle."

(Above, Laurence Square circa the early 1930s, probably not long after the traffic rotary was installed. Photo, Collection of the Torrington Historical Society.)

Responses included: "I remember that traffic circle well. We lived nearby and my sister went to kindergarten at North School right there." . . . "From this view, would the police station be on the right, or do I have the location wrong?" (Answer = You have it right.)

Post: The 1964 THS Band & Mr. Wheeler

Let's hear it for the THS band, in this particular case the 1964 musicians (pictured below). Too often the bulk of the publicity in a school goes to the athletes first, then the scholars, then perhaps the thespians, and probably lastly the musicians, at least of those groups in the public eye. Looking the 1964 band over (below), I see Rich

Coralli, John Hass, and John Dohanyos front-and-center. Spread around the room, in no particular order, there are Steve Dohanyos, Sharon Anderson, Alan Rosa, Lorraine Allyn, Jim Juralewicz, Paul Arezzini, Jane Conforti, Robert Britton, Pete Froeliger, Lou Troccolo, and so many others including beloved band director David Wheeler in the upper right rear corner. . . I auditioned for the band freshman year, two years before this, then decided 5 years of B-flat clarinet was enough. The music loving public (mainly my family) was thrilled.

Responses included: "I went into the band room one day to help someone move something, and sat down and played the piano. Mr. Wheeler came in and kicked me out because if you weren't in the band, you had no business touching the instruments. Sad part was that I was better than the regular piano player." . . . "Mr. Wheeler was a great guy. But oh, those tired old band uniforms!" . . .

"Wheeler was a good guy. But like most teachers back then, he played it pretty close to the rule book/hand book. He loved to blast the volume in Music Appreciation class." . . . "Yeah, Wheeler was a nice guy. I told him I never joined the band because I thought it would be too hard to carry an organ or piano in a parade. I played accordion too." . . . "Mr. Wheeler was not only a talented musician, but he was also an amateur astronomer, and in later years built his own telescope and went around to the schools and various local groups giving lectures and classes on astronomy. I believe he brought his telescope along." . . . "David Wheeler was also a woodworker. He built a wooden boat, probably to sail away from the students."

(Below, a May 2, 1964 clipping from *The Torrington Register*.)

MEMORIAL TRUMPET, given in memory of Charlotte Wendt, Torrington High School sophomore who died last year of cancer, was presented to Robert Gallo, solo trumpeter in high school band, at assembly held yesterday at the school. Trumpet will remain in the band and will be used each year by solo trumpeter.

In photo are, left to right: first row — David Wheeler, supervisor of music, making presentation; Gallo, Lorraine Allyn, Stephen Dohanyos and Louis Troccolo; second row — Anthony Picone, John Haas, John Dohanyos, Charles Swanson and John Coard.

Post: 1960, the Iolanthe Production and Ethel Johnson

Love this picture (below). It was entitled, "Waiting their cues for

Iolanthe" in the 1960 THS yearbook. That's Bob White in the center surrounded by a bevy of leading females. Cast members included Joanne Fischer, Marion Nierintz, Evelyn Perugini, Stuart Cohen, Marlene Buccos, Robert Cleaveland, Marianne Gelormino, and Judith Navalanic. The director was David Wheeler, and Ethel Johnson was in charge of production. Though I was never in a play, and back in high school never really cared much for them (a genuine philistine boob), the old Melpothalian Dramatic Club and Thespian Troupe #611 put on many fine productions. . . I also love this picture because it shows the old auditorium well. Despite the hard, wooden seats, it was a room with character.

Responses included: "In 1967, Ethel Johnson, who had directed many plays over the years, was retiring. She was also adviser to the Thespians, and we put on a retirement party for her. It was at the Torringford Grange, and I'm pretty sure it was a surprise. The location and the surprise aspect were planned with her family (her brother was Clarence Johnson of Mason & Johnson, and her sister Ruth was married to Phil Hewitt, salesman at Greene Ford Sales - they were all Torringford people). The then-current crop of THS actors put on a program of scenes from about 8 of the plays she had directed. There was a sign that said "ELJ PRODUCTIONS." I remember we did scenes from *Our Town, A Midsummer Night's Dream, Outward Bound*, and, I think, *Teahouse Of The August Moon*. She was thrilled. She, and her colleagues Frances Barrett and William Muller, and of course teachers before and after my time that I never knew, introduced us to a wide variety of plays. We did *Medea*, Moliere's *The Imaginary Invalid, Green Grow The Lilacs, Arsenic and Old Lace, HMS Pinafore*, and a children's fantasy *The Land Of The Dragon* that the elementary school kids were brought to see. I thank Miss Johnson for my lifelong love of the theater."

(Above, English teacher Ethel Johnson in her classroom, 1962.)

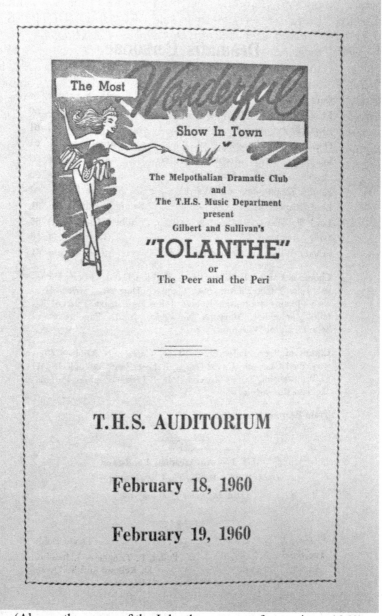

(Above, the cover of the Iolanthe program from winter 1960)

Post: Herbie Lehmann

Herbie Lehmann was in the THS Class Of 1959. When I was in high school, he ran the pool hall Central Billiards on Water Street and later ran the world famous Ames in NYC (where *The Hustler* was shot). Herbie was a GREAT pool player, a national caliber talent who competed in 10 world pool tournaments and won more than his fair share of accolades. For many years he installed and maintained pool tables throughout the New England, New York area, and today he can be frequently seen walking the streets of Torrington (Above right, near Vogel-Wetmore) for exercise. He has the aura and gait of a much younger man. Herbie has always had a touch of class with a patina of worldliness, i.e. a standout in our borough, and it's been a pleasure to know him all these years.

Responses included: "He once beat me for an hour straight in 9-ball. I shot my regular not-too-bad game. Herbie shot left-handed and had to bank all his shots. I never came close to winning." . . . "Herbie is also quite a dancer. Danced all night at our 50th Reunion. Hope to see him this fall at our 60th." . . . "I remember he used to like jazz a lot." . . . "I knew Herbie Lehman from the time I was about 8-years-old, maybe even a little younger. I used to play pool when Henry (Burnell) was running the place, and, of course, I stayed on after Herbie took over. Because I've known Herbie for so long he took a little extra interest in showing me the game. Unfortunately I didn't have his drive and I never really mastered it. But I had a good time." . . . "Herbie served in the Army in Vietnam as a cook. I believe he tried his hand at being a cook in civilian life after that, but he eventually went back to the real love of his life - billiards." . . . "I spent a lot of time at his pool hall on Water Street. I won a tournament and had my picture in the paper, to which my mother replied, 'Oh great. Now everyone will know that you hang around in a pool hall.' She *did* like the trophy though."

Post: Addo and Ezio Bonetti

The mason and politician (on the left in the below picture) with the teacher and coach (on the right). I took this picture of the Bonetti brothers, Addo and Ezio, around the mid-1990s at Fuessenich Park. Great guys, both of them. Addo was in the THS Class Of 1945, while Ezio was in the Class Of 1942. **Memories**: Ezio hit a softball once in PE that STILL might be going. I remember him in later years telling me about the death of his wife, and I remember how he started to cry. It was very shocking to me (since we didn't know each other that well), *but* it was also very moving. . . Addo, one of the most well liked politicians Torrington has ever had. Addo used to drive his payloader up to the corner of Homestead and Allen Road in the big snow storms and rearrange the snow banks. When we were neighbors for 20 years, he generously let me dump sticks and leaves, i.e. yard waste, on his property. I'd phone him occasionally to get information/insight/a quote on local matters and people, and he never failed to provide input. Two memorable and great people.

Responses included: "Great guys. I remember that when I was in high school, Ezio used to drive an orangy-red MGA (that is if my memory is at all accurate)." . . . "Addo was my Little League coach, and Ezio was my teacher *and* track and football coach. Used Ezio as my subject for an essay as part of a college admission application." . . . "Addo was our Little League coach and also a volunteer fireman, so when a fire was called in, he left. Had many golf matches against Ezio. We all thought his handicap was a bit suspect. Both were great guys." . . . "Great photo of two outstanding people. Addo was among the first coaches in Torrington's Little League. Careful shaking his hand; he will crush you! Ezio, a well-know track coach at THS, but few know that he excelled at baseball and, I believe, played professionally. These are two that I would love to sit with and have a drink and some conversation." . . . "I never had the chance to meet Addo, but I knew Ezio pretty well and liked him very much. He was a good guy. Told me how some runners excel in the cold and don't do as well in the heat. (me). I asked him to make track a winter sport. He said they run cross country in the fall. This was before the jogging craze of the mid-'70s." . . . "Ezio's strong point was in getting some really outstanding people out for the team and motivating them to practice and excel. His coaching knowledge was best in baseball, and his '75 THS team won a state title." . . . "Hats off for two fantastic men. Let's not forget, the service Addo gave to our great country. He was a Marine Corps veteran, a 'graduate' of Parris Island, and had fought at Iwo Jima." . . . "Addo is still his usual cheerful self and despite some medical problems has come around quite nicely. He's elated with the fact that he is still able to drive. You might catch him on the road waving and sporting that signature smile. I visited his home on Homestead Lane many times since he initially purchased it. He loves every minute there and works diligently to improve the property. He loves assisting his neighbors even more. He bestowed the same kindness to his neighbors when he lived in the South End, always being on his tractor while crossing the bridge to be of assistance to anyone plowed in. He is a rare and special breed. I could go on forever about the many kindnesses that he has shown to so many, but knowing Addo, he would 'Shush' me. However, people might be interested in Addo's brave actions during the flood of '55. Also, during any blizzard, instead of being in the comfort of his home, the amazing Mr. Addo Bonetti will be in his truck endlessly navigating Torrington's streets to assist anyone in need - day and night. I have said too much. On a Cappuccino high." (Right, a vintage pinback. Addo was elected and re-elected *many* times.)

FULL TIME
CITY CLERK
ADDO
VOTE
DEMOCRATIC

Post: Nellie Sullivan

So it's the first week of school my senior year and during the lunch block I have a study hall once a week on the first floor of A building. Nellie Sullivan is the monitor. I get a pass to go to the library (which is on the second floor of B building). When I get there she's waiting at the door. My reaction is surprise along the lines of WTF? She asks where I've been, what route I took. I tell her I walked through the caf (wanted to check out the scene). She tells me I should have taken the A-B connector, that it's the faster route. Then she tells me she's pulling my passes FOR THE YEAR! Grounds me. For my entire senior year. Not even lav privileges. All because she beat me to the library by a minute. . . Nellie Sullivan.

(Above, Nellie Sullivan in 1962. Few students ever saw this smile.)

Responses included: "Well, that is something else a school could never do today. Schools were their own kingdoms in our day." . . . "Never did like Nellie Sullivan - or that other crab who taught home economics. I forget her name." . . . "What a petty tyrant. That dumb-arse was a Guidance Counselor (remember?). She told my brother

that his ideal career would be as an undertaker. Sheet-for-brains." . . .
"She told me I would never get into college, let alone graduate. I'd
love to wave my Bachelor's and Master's degrees in her face! What a
poor excuse for a 'guidance' counselor!" . . . "I'm in Sullivan's study
hall, and first marking period ends. She tells us put our report cards
on top of our desks. We're puzzled, but who ever argued with Nellie
Sullivan! She starts with the first row by the windows, first seat.
Picks up each report card individually, and comments on it to the
entire study hall. Goes through every student in the room. The good
report cards get a positive comment and a metaphorical pat on the
head. Unfortunately many in this study hall are not sweet
conscientious students. These report cards get comments along the
lines: 'this is a disgrace,' 'wait till your parents see this,' 'you're not
going to graduate,' 'how could you flunk that simple course,' etc.
Danny sits in front of me. Sullivan verbally castrates him and leaves
him bloodied and psychically wounded. Second marking period
ends. Danny is the third one she gets to. 'Where's your report card?'
she asks tapping his desk. 'You're not going to see it,' he says and
adds, 'You have no right. You're only a study hall teacher.' Steam
rises from Nellie Sullivan; her face is red with fury. But she says
nothing and moves on. I'm next. 'You're not seeing mine either,' I say
looking her squarely in the eyes. She moves on. Half a dozen others
refuse to show her their report cards. The rebellion grows and by 4th
marking period she doesn't ask to see them." . . . "Nellie told my
parents not to bother with me. That I never tried. That I wasn't worth
the trouble or the money. Thankfully my parents loved me enough to
bother." . . . "True story. During the summer before my senior year, I
attended a basketball camp in upper New York state. Two of the
coaches that were in attendance were West Point head coach Bob
Knight and West Point assistant coach Mike Krzyzewski. I had a
pretty good camp and, on the last day they both came up to me
saying they would be in touch. I didn't think much of it because there
was no way I was West Point material and who were they, anyway?
A couple of months into my senior season Nellie Sullivan pulled me
out of my English class and yelled at me saying, 'Who do you think
you are applying to West Point?' and showed me the application
packet sent by West Point along with hand-written letters from both
coaches. She proceeded to rip the the application forms and the
coaches letters. In reality, no hard feelings. She was who she was!" . .
. "I hated Nellie Sullivan. She gave me a D in algebra. I got As in
college. So much for her teaching abilities." . . . "I hate to say this,
but that is part of what is missing in our society today: discipline and

respect for authority. Ninety-nine percent of the kids turned out all right as far as I can see in spite of the Nellie Sullivans of the world. Someone dared me on the second day of my freshman year to call Mr. Ezio Bonetti by his first name. Of course, I never passed up a dare, which resulted in two weeks of detention at Fuessenich Park doing laps around the track and going up-and-down the bleacher stairs. We learned to respect our elders. Got us ready for marriage."

Postscript: Nellie Sullivan died in November 1994. She was 79. She was a graduate of THS and Marywood College in Pennsylvania. She began teaching at THS in 1936 and over the years taught math, Latin, and English. She was a guidance counselor for 11 years and retired in 1974. She was quoted in *The Torrington Register* as saying the

reason she became a guidance counselor was, "I like students and the counseling setup provides a much more relaxed contact. It's more free and intimate than the classroom relationship." Her obituary said she spent 10 summers and many Christmas breaks doing volunteer work in the ghettos of Chicago. After she retired she spent a year in the Christian Appalachian Project, volunteering as a cook for poor children. Still later she was a patient care volunteer for Hospice and Visiting Nurses. . . Her obit doesn't mesh nicely with most students' experiences with her, i.e. she seems to have had a real dual nature, not given to easy stereotyping. . . Most former Red Raiders today *still* cannot think fondly of her, though perhaps she did not think fondly of herself. In any case, RIP Nellie Sullivan.

(Below, a news clipping from the February 2, 1972, issue of *The Torrington Register*.)

Honored by Probus

Miss Nellie J. Sullivan, a Torrington High School teacher for 26 years and guidance counselor for the past nine years, has been designated as recipient of the 17th annual Probus Club "Educator of the Year" award. The plaque will be presented at a dinner meeting in the spring.

Post: Abernethy's Store

One of my absolute favorite pieces of Torrington memorabilia is a large, framed painting of Abernethy's Store (below). It was a gift to

me from Geri Spino last September. Geri is the widow of Rollie Spino, and together they owned Spino's Men's Wear in the Mertz building from 1979 -2008. This painting hung in their store for decades, and after Spino's closed, the painting hung in their house. They knew how much I liked it, and before Rollie passed he told Geri he wanted me to have it. VERY generous of him, and I could not have been more thrilled when out-of-the-blue Geri phoned last year with the gift offer. She even arranged for neighbor Addo Bonetti to deliver it. . . Abernethy's store was built in 1803 by Russell Abernethy. It was located on the corner of Hodges Hill Road and University Drive. It was the child of the department store later to be called The W.W. Mertz Co. In 1825 Russell Abernethy moved his store downtown from University Drive, and for the next 150+ years it went through a succession of names, owners, and buildings. . . Enjoy this brief look back to when the hub of Torrington activity and the town green were on University Drive, back when the downtown area was a swamp. And let's give thanks to Rollie and Geri Spino for creating this painting and helping to keep a part of Mertz going for 30+ years.

Responses included: "Thank you to the Spinos. I have many fond memories of Mertz from my childhood." . . . "I'd never heard of Abernethy's before." . . . "I doubt many have. But if you lived on the West Side of town 200+ years ago, let's say in the Wright's, University Drive, Klug Road area, this was a place you went to to shop and socialize." . . . "I'm not certain, and I could be wrong, but I believe that Rollie had at one point in time worked at the Quality Hat Store and then later on, at the Sears Men's Wear when they were on the Winsted Road.. This was prior to opening his own store in the Mertz building." . . . "Looking at the picture brings to mind John Brown's birthplace (pictured on our old blue recycle tubs) which was in this neighborhood." . . . "Was that time, 1800, before the factories were built in town and on the rivers and dams?" . . . "Our industrialized life was just about to start. The first factory was probably a woolen mill in the downtown/Wolcottville area around where lower Water Street is today. That mill was built in 1813."

(Above, the intersection of Hodges Hill Road going down to the left and University Drive going south on the right towards the Goshen Road. This is where Abernethy's store stood over 200 years ago.)

Post: Roland "Rollie" Spino

I'm greatly saddened by the passing of Roland "Rollie" Spino earlier this week. He was a member of the THS Class of 1949, a terrific athlete, a successful Torrington businessman (worked at Quality Hat and later owned Spino's Men's Shop), a well known and well liked man-about-town, and a neighbor of mine for 20 years. He's one of those people I wish I'd written an article on, but the one time he agreed to it I was taking a break from writing. And the other times I asked, his modesty wouldn't allow it. . . The pictures here all come from Rollie. These and many more he shared with me. I believe they capture a bygone Torrington. And I'm most grateful to Rollie for having the foresight to take and to save them. And to share them with me, and now with us. . .

(Above, THS freshman basketball team, NVL champs in 1946. Back Row, L-R: Coach Lindahl, Carillo, Ernie Pollack, Eagan, Salvatore Julian, Frank Stolfi, Faillace. . . Front Row: Sam Mele, John Fox, Domenic "Sonny" Toce, Co-captain Rollie Spino, Co-captain Alphonese Gautieri, Andy Hricko, Stan Nawalaniec, Manager William Toussaint.)

Responses included: "Rollie was a great guy. I bought a lot of clothes from him over the years." . . . "Top notch. Absolutely the best. I too purchased clothes from him. I still wear the topcoat he sold me when I 'dress up.' " . . . "Another Torrington legend has left us!" . . . "Rollie was one of those rare people I never heard a negative or harsh word about. People just truly liked the guy, and respected the man." . . . "He used to help me pick out presents for my boy friends. I was a big spender, sweaters usually. Such a friendly and kind man." . . . "I saw Rollie a couple of times this winter working out at the YMCA. He always took a lot of pride in staying in shape." . . . "I worked at Quality Hat Store. A really good group of people, but I especially enjoyed working with Rollie. We had lots of laughs. And of course there was his never ending sense of humor, often at my expense." . . . "Rollie was the baby of the Spino family of ten children; only two are left. He was a good man and will be missed by all of us who loved him dearly." . . . "I feel blessed to have spoken to Rollie at church the previous Sunday before he died. Such a wonderful and special person. May he rest in peace."

(Above, the staff of Quality Hat Store, 1964: L-R: JD Palmer [from Texas], Hubbard, Jim Marine [owner, tall, glasses], Anita Marine [in front of husband], Chester Goldstein, Shirley Clapps, Rollie Spino, Pete Riley.)

Post: Teacher Appreciation

During this May's Teacher Appreciation Week at THS, students were allowed to post sticky note tributes to the teachers. These were stuck on the glass on both sides of the corridor in the old A-B connector (Picture below), and have been left up. You don't have to read many to get the overwhelming impression that the current THS faculty and student body have a VERY good rapport. A few of the succinct postings include: Ms. Magistrali and Ms. Stomski are amazing! School nurses, thanks for letting me nap! Mr. S you have an amazing voice, plus I love the puns! Mr. C, Homeland Security got nothing on you! Mrs. Sullivan, the funniest, most caring teacher ever! et al. . . Question: Had this tradition been in place when we were school back in the 1950s, '60s, and '70s, what teacher would *you* have cited AND what would you have said?. . .

Responses included: "Mrs. Barrett, because her tests were so inventive. Write an essay on gray, she once said, so I wrote one on a prison. I could just as easily written about a lovely gray skirt, or *The Grey Fairy Book* by Charles Perreault. She was also very kind to me, and warm, in a New England way." . . . "I would have said Mrs. Barrett too. Her class was always interesting, and she was so nice to everyone." . . . "Mr. Urda, who was instrumental in getting me to focus on science and engineering. And his classroom demonstrations were pretty cool, too." . . . "Bill Meyer, who sparked my interest in biology so that I majored in bio in college and taught high school biology for several years!" . . . "Miss Zaharek was by far the teacher that saved my life in high school, and with a simple gesture that she wouldn't have thought twice about. At a time when my life was upside down and I had zero self-esteem, a simple thing like a teacher putting their hand on my shoulder and saying I was good in math gave me hope and turned my life around! It's something I have never forgotten! I wonder how many of us have given a word of encouragement to some unbeknowing soul that changed their lives and we were clueless, probably very much like Miss Zaharek!" . . . "Mrs. Svetz - She made my love for sewing blossom! To this day, I remember tips that she gave me when constructing a garment, and every time I'm at my sewing machine, I think of her. God rest her soul." . . . "Maria Cravanzola, Doris Polastri, and Maureen Shugrue (three caring women who refused to let me go down the wrong road). Also, Henry Pavlak, Cliff Mignerey, Miss Zaharek, Sy Franklin, Mr. Pudlinski, Big George Urda, and Chuck Fador - big thanks to each of them."

Frances Barrett, English Dept. Head

At a Board of Education meeting held Monday night, Mrs. Frances D. Barrett was appointed head of the English department to replace Mr. Tracey Conway.

Mrs. Barrett graduated from Albertus Magnus College where she majored in English literature and composition. She first taught in Thomaston, and then in Harwinton, and has been a member of the faculty for the past ten years.

Among her extra activities, she serves as secretary of the Goshen Board of Education of which she has been a member for sixteen years. The Goshen Players also count her among their charter members, and she is a member of the Democratic Town Committee in Goshen.

(Above, a front page article from the December 1966 issue of the school newspaper *The X Ray*. Because Frances Barrett received more tributes than any other teacher [I didn't include them all.], she's more than deserving of revisiting her picture and headline.)

Post: Teen Memories

For sure, I thought the teen, carefree, THS years would last forever while they were going on. I think most teens do, part of youth's shortsightedness. . . So, anyone care to share an outstanding memory from those years that you thought would last forever? Mine would be the night as a freshman I was standing outside the Farm Shop on a winter night, and a car pulled up. Vic Radzevich rolled down the window and said, "Bentley, get in the back. You're going drinking with us." Ray Pollick was driving, and the three of us tooled up to

West Hill and pulled over where Brodie Park is today. We each had a beer, maybe two, and that was my initiation into underage, high school drinking. I still today in 2019 think of those guys as cool, though I haven't seen either in decades.

(Left, Fuessenich Park, 1963. Track coach Ezio Bo-netti clowns around with Co-captain Vic Radzevich, by sticking a starter gun into his co-captain's ribs. Imagine doing this today.)

<u>Responses included</u>: "I was out riding around with Sheik. I made a comment that he didn't like, and he put me out of the car someplace close to Litchfield. Thankfully he relented, and I didn't have to walk home." . . . "I remember the first time I went to the Tally Ho. I heard the older guys talking about it for a couple of years, and it seemed like it was the size of Disney World. When we pulled into the parking lot, my first reaction was, 'Okay, where is it?' Quite a letdown, but the beer was good." . . . "How about the For and Aft? It was right over the state line off I-84. Great dance floor and pinball machines before they became electronic." . . . "The wise guys would sometimes put a cherry bomb down a toilet in the boys lav. It'd go off and shake up the nearby classrooms. Then the lav would flood and it'd be closed down for awhile. Big inconvenience. Of course there were student patrol people, and you were supposed to sign in-and-out of the lav, so theoretically it shouldn't have been hard to find the culprit. I think they usually did. Duggan was good at that sort of thing. The bomber would be talked about, and even if he got kicked out of school for awhile, he'd be sort of a THS hero, at least at Scarp's where those sorts hung out." . . . "Still happy and grateful for those wonderful years of learning, laughing, and friendships. Would not change anything about those years. Loved going to the Y for Friday night dances, hanging at The Farm Shop and Wright's. And, of course, there was always Thursday night shopping back when downtown was jumping!" . . . "I puked once at the Tally Ho and then went back in to drink more." . . . "We girls went to the bars in New York State too. I remember the most popular drinks were Whiskey Sours, Sloe Gin Fizzes, and Singapore Slings, though we'd drink beer too. One of the girls I hung around with looked older. She'd put her hair in curlers and go into First National and buy us beer. I don't think she ever got carded."

(Above, a member of the THS Class Of 1967 clowns around for a yearbook photo. The theme was booze and tobacco, i.e. popular teen taboos.)

Post: Luis Thuillard and His 53-year-old Record

Perhaps today's Torrington headline should read: "Seventy Year Old Man Breaks High School Record." Backstory: There's a large track & field record board on the back of the THS gym. The oldest Red Raider record on that board is from Luis "The Cat" Thuillard who, according to the record board, threw the shot 54'10¼" in 1966. That distance always seemed correct to me, never gave it a second thought. THEN, yesterday I stumbled across a small article from June 1966 (On left). According to the short piece, Lu took 3rd in the State Meet in the shot put and threw 56'2¼" - almost a foot-and-a-half farther than his own record on the Raider board. Was it true? I went on the State Library website and went into the *Hartford Courant* archives. Found the article on the '66 state meet. Yes, Lu had taken third, but no distance was given. Should I contact the CIAC? Seemed like jumping into a bottomless bureaucratic pit. Sooooo, I got Lu's number and phoned

Lou Thuillard Breaks Record

Torrington High's Lu Thuillard, breaking the school record in the shot put, placed third in the Connecticut track and field finals Saturday at Yale University.

Lu, whose school record-breaking effort was measured at 56 feet, 2¼ inches, will travel to Keene, N. H., Saturday to represent Connecticut in the New England finals.

First place in Saturday's shot put event went to Bruce Wentworth of East Hartford, with a distance of 59 feet, 3½ inches.

him. We hadn't spoken since probably our THS days (don't recall ever seeing him after graduation), but it was like old times. The half century evaporated. Yes, Lu said, he DID throw 56'2¼" in the state meet. No, he said, I didn't know that my record was incorrectly cited/ listed on the record board and in the THS record books. . . I contacted THS AD (athletic director). No problem, he said, the change will be made. . . So, today's headline, as far as I'm concerned,

is, "Seventy Year Old Man Breaks High School Record." . . . Just one thing more - there are at least 2 other records that are incorrectly cited on the Raider board, that haven't been updated in over a year. So I hope Lu's not in any hurry. . .

(Right, Lu Thuillard in 1966 gets ready to launch the 12-pound shot.)

Responses included: "Good work! Lu is such a great guy and an amazing athlete. Thanks for your brilliant detective work and setting the past straight." . . . "He lived in my neighborhood around East Pearl Park and played in all of our pick up games in all 3 sports." . . . "Wish he would join Facebook and this THS page, or at least go to a reunion. But for whatever reason, I don't think either will happen." . . . "Luis is quite a guy!" . . . "He was a great athlete and deserves the notoriety." . . . "Just now I realize how French his name looks, but I knew that Spanish was his first language." . . . "His first name is Luis. His last name is from his Swiss father." . . . "Thanks for tracking (pun intended) down the facts. Lu is a great guy!"

Post: Helen Woodford

Helen Woodford was one of the girls' physical education teachers. She was also, eventually, the department head. My wife tells me that she told Ms. Woodford that she was feeling sick one day when they were on the playing fields, and Woodford growled at her to go into the woods if she wanted to throw up.

Responses included: "Whoa! I haven't had my coffee yet!" . . . "I don't know that I want to remember! LOL." . . . "The one memory I still have of Ms. Woodford was her handing me a towel as I ran (as fast as I could) through the girls' shower after P. E. You know, Ms. Woodford, I could have gotten my own towel, thank you very much!" . . . "I don't remember ever seeing her smile like in this picture! She was a pretty scary woman, but I bet she loved her job being a teacher." . . . "She looks so sweet and cute in this picture! Not the lady I remember!" . . . "I ended up taking care of her at the assisted living place on the Goshen Road. You should have seen her then when she was 80. Now that was scary!" . . . "I felt like she

Bentley   The Torrington & THS FB Posts

wanted to see us naked. Yuk!" . . . "The only P. E. teacher worse than Ms. Woodford was Ms. Trost, who was from the South and had a wicked Southern accent. I admit I was a troublemaker in her class because I imitated her accent, and she later gave me a poor grade because of this. I told my father she marked me down for having dirty gym socks - as if my meticulous Italian mother would ever have sent me to school with anything dirty!"

Postscript: Bloomfield native Helen Woodford died there in July 2015. She was 88-years-old. She had degrees from the University Of Bridgeport and the University Of Hartford. She taught in Torrington for 34 years. Her obituary read in part: "The Girl Scouts were near and dear to Helen, and she held a variety of positions including Girl Scout Camp Director for a few years. She volunteered her multiple talents to a variety of organizations including the Sullivan Senior Center, the Community Kitchen, United Congregational Church, and the American Cancer Society." She was survived by 2 sisters.

(Right, Helen Woodford in 1965 looking very stylish in a blazer and yet with the ever present PE whistle around her neck, prepares to play some LPs on a portable record player.)

29

Post: The Antique Car Caravan or Best To Stay In Torrington

It's true. Some people have no manners, more specifically a whole bunch of vintage car owners. . . Backstory: Beautiful day today, pretty much perfect, so Karen and I decide to go for a bike ride on the Harlem Valley Rail Trail in Millerton, NY. The trail is 40-45 minutes away, and it's a lovely ride through the heart of NW CT. It's also generally a fast ride, since despite the fact that it's mainly composed of secondary highways, the traffic is almost always light. . . We leave the house at 8:30, and take Rt. 4 to the Goshen rotary. No problems. Traffic moving fast like the drivers are oblivious to speed limit signs and the possibility of radar guns pointed their way. Turn north at the rotary onto Rt. 63 but not far past the town "center" have to apply the brakes. Slow moving cars ahead. A line of them. Vintage Cadillac convertible in front of me, an old MG in front of him, then 10-12 antique Model Ts. My first impulse is to start passing, but there are simply too many of them on this windy and hilly road to ever hope to get past them all. So I settle back. The caravan is going 40 mph tops, and many times 30-35. I'm getting frustrated. A long line of cars forms behind me. It finally dawns on me that these 12-14 antiques are probably a car club headed to Lime Rock. Big weekend at the race track, and must be a car show too. Damn bit of bad luck for us civilian bikers. . . Slowly the convoy eats up the miles. I'm praying they're going to Canaan or points north, maybe to participate in a parade. Fingers crossed, swear words at a minimum. Then we hit the Rt. 126 turnoff towards Falls Village (and Lime Rock and Millerton), and all the turn signals come on. Double damn. I next hope that maybe a top-heavy Model T or two falls over on the turn so the others will have to pull over and let us civilians pass. But no such luck. They continue to mosey-on-down-the-road. Next I hope they don't know about the Johnson Road shortcut to the left, but yeah they do. Triple DAMN! I put the pedal-to-the-metal once they've all turned and zoom straight ahead, speed limit go-to-hell. At the intersection with Rt. 7 in Falls Village (Torrington Savings Bank on the right), I take a left and continue my high speed attempt to cut off the crawling convoy. We'll intersect a couple of miles down the road when they too hit Rt. 7. Will I make it? Will I avoid a speeding ticket? Answers arrive in two minutes. Good News: No speeding ticket. Bad News: Three model Ts beat us and get onto Rt. 7 just ahead of us. Just 3, but might as well be a dozen on this serpentine road. Just past Housatonic Valley High School the trio turn right onto Rt. 112 towards Lime Rock (and Millerton). I'd give the three a damn x 4, but Karen reminds me that the race track is getting very close and to JUST BE PATIENT!. . . Finally we get to Lime Rock, and yes, there's a car show. And yes, the three turn in. As I zip past the last one, I give a lengthy horn blast. Karen's eyes go up, and she asks, Does that make you feel better? I say, Yeah, it does, and I smile. Damn inconsiderate vintage car owners, but it's a gorgeous day, so I put them literally behind me. Good News: There are no vintage cars and practically no traffic at all on the return trip home. Guess they finally pulled over for the day. . .

Responses included: "You're retired and can ride your bike anytime. Why pick a weekend?" . . . Was anyone breaking the law? Slow down and enjoy the ride." . . . "OMG! One of those antique drivers just told me that he kept looking in his rearview mirror and thinking, 'Those people are going to kill us!' " . . . "If anyone knows who these drivers are, give them my name. I can tell them how to travel the roads properly, not hold up traffic, and *still* arrive at Lime Rock together." . . . "Pretty funny. Most seniors complain about drivers going too *fast*. LOL."

(Above. Main Street car show, spring 2019. A vintage auto sits in front of the Torrington Historical Society, a fitting location for the classic car. Rhetorical Question: Did it arrive here singularly *or* in a slow moving caravan?. . .)

Post: They Died While In The Service

As you all know, Memorial Day 2019 is a time for honoring those who died while serving in the United States Armed Forces. Though not related to combat and not in Vietnam, the deaths of 3 Torrington natives and THS grads: Clifford Mignerey (died in 1967), Alfred "Skip" Eyre (1968), and Dennis Novak (1970) all came at a time when these young men were honorably in uniform. . . First Lt. Clifford Mignerey (Right, in 1961) was killed near Fort Rucker, Alabama, late in his Army flight training. He was airborne and preparing to make a message drop when his plane crashed and burned. He was awarded his Army aviator wings posthumously. . . Skip Eyre was in the Navy and died when his car crashed into a utility pole 10 miles north of Key West, Florida. He was 18-years-old. . . Airman 1st Class Dennis Novak was

stationed at Kadena Air Force Base, Okinawa. He died following a brief illness. Novak was 19-years-old. . . Let us take a few moments today to remember all three, to share any memories of them, and to remember what bright shining lights they were when they were with us.

Responses included: "I remember these deaths distinctly. I did not know Skip Eyre, but I knew his dad from the golf course and his mom from shopping at Stop 'n Save. I believe Clifford Mignerey may have been a counselor at Camp Workcoeman in the mid-1960s." . . . "I knew Dennis Novak from high school. He may been the first person to die from the Class Of 1969. (Right, Dennis Novak in 1969) I believe his father had a plumbing business. I remember Skip Eyre. (Below, Skip Eyre in 1967) He was my sister's age, and his father and mine were in The Lion's Club together. We attended a few Lion's banquets together. He was a funny guy! He was the first young person I knew who died. RIP" . . . "My mother was a friend of Clifford Mignerey's mother, and Trinity Church is where I remember Cliff from,

though I can't say I knew him personally. I remember how shocking and sad his death was." . . . "I knew Cliff Mignerey from the YMCA swim team and Trinity Church where he was an altar boy. I always thought of him as the ideal teen, i.e. clean cut, handsome, and involved in the right activities." . . . "When I was a teenager I was a sitter for Skip and his sister Jane. Great kiddos." . . . "Skip Eyre's high school class of 1967 was broken up by his passing, as were many of us who knew him to be a carefree and constantly smiling guy."

Post: Warner Theatre Memories

I was walking on Main Street 2 days ago around 9 a.m. and was struck by how terrific the old ticket/box "office" at the Warner looked. There was a vintage radio behind the glass, original marquee

numbers that spelled out "1931" (the year the Warner opened), some used art-deco projection reels, lighting filters, and other pieces of authentic Warner memorabilia. It all brought back a flood of memories. So many movies, cartoons, newsreels; so many Saturday and Sunday afternoons spent in the dark warm confines of the art deco house. Was there a better place to see *Ben-Hur, Bridge on the River Kwai, Godzilla, Attack of the 50 Foot Woman, Old Yeller*, and so much more, including graduations, beauty pageants, etc. What are your own fond Warner memories these 2019 days?

Responses included: "I remember going to the movies every Tuesday evening with my mom to get the free place settings. We

34

didn't buy dishes for years!" . . . "Strawberry Alarm Clock concert -
maybe 1966?" . . . "Very first movie I ever saw there was Disney's *Cinderella*. I think the last movie I saw there was *Jaws*." . . . "Had many dance recitals there." . . . "Seeing *Rodan* with my big brother, and *Around The World In 80 Days* with my mother, both 1956 films." . . . "Sitting through *A Hard Days*

Night several times over in one afternoon." . . . "Going to see Elvis movies!" . . . "Saturday afternoons meant two movies, a serial, and cartoons. My Dad would give me fifty cents, and it got me in and enough left over for treats." . . . "Sneaking into the balcony as a kid!" . . . "Sneaking in from the left side of the theater from that alley that was there." . . . "Sunday afternoon, latest sci-fi for 35 cents back in the '50s, early '60s. Then coming out and finding Sam the Hot Dog man selling those salty hot dogs." . . . "My first job was there behind the candy counter. Many fond memories!" . . . "Many concerts and dance recitals that both my daughter and I were a part of!" . . . "Some time in the early '60s, going on stage to dance while Freddy 'Boom Boom' Cannon sang 'Palisades Park.' We all got a voucher for free food at Tony's." . . . "Going to the Sunday double feature in 6th/7th grade and hoping by the 2nd movie one of the girls would come and sit next to me in the back row. Besides that, walking to the theatre for the Saturday afternoon horror/monster feature straight down Main Street from Margerie Street. I was 6 and 7-years-old at the time going to the movies by myself in 1958/'59. Can you imagine that now? The gray haired lady at the Warner was scary." . . . "I remember as a kid going to my older sister's THS graduation at the Warner in the early 1960s. I sat in the back of the balcony, and the people on stage seemed far away. Couldn't see anything very well. I remember the class sang 'You'll Never Walk Alone' at the end of the ceremony. It was very moving, even for a kid."

(Above, a 1944 THS graduation ticket for the ceremony at the Warner. Ticket compliments of Mary and Don Schroeder.)

"I remember going to concerts with my mom. They were put on by the Torrington Men's Chorus - a really good group in its day - and always featured some well-known performer. I remember Dick Liebert on organ, and William Warfield, famous for his rendition of 'Old Man River' in the movie *Showboat*. I think Roger Williams, too, but cannot be sure." . . . "I remember it cost 25 cents to see two movies and cartoons." . . . "Many memories. First movie I ever saw (with my parents) was *Song of the South*. I remember as a young kid going to see musicals with our visiting grandmother, later as high school senior going to Friday night shows after work (work was in the credit department of Sears, Roebuck, located on south side of lower East Main), and, finally, having our graduation ceremony there!" . . . "I remember the Vagabonds putting on an indoor drum corps show at the Warner. Really lit the place up!" . . . "At least three times a year these 2019 days when I work at the Warner, someone asks me if the balcony is upstairs. I usually tell them that we tried moving it but it wasn't the same." . . . "Regular movies cost 25 cents and Disney movies were 50 cents. Remember seeing *Psycho* in 1960 with Cheryl (we were only ten years old then), and I've never been the same in the shower since! My mother didn't know how violent the film was, or she never would have let me go. It was winter and nighttime, and when we got out, a blizzard was starting. Cheryl's father gave me a ride home, and I was so scared to get out of the car, I made sure he waited until I got inside. That film still scares me to this day!"

(Right, an ad from a July 1960 issue of *The Torrington Register*.)

Post: T.H.S. Graduation Memories

As high school graduations wind down, I can't help thinking of my own THS graduation in 1966. (Right, a 1966 graduation tassel.) It was a hot June evening, and the high school gym was sweltering. Steam heat. I have MANY memories of that night - before, during, and after the ceremony. But a simple one that stands out is the fact that I saw classmates cross the stage that night that I swear I hadn't seen in 4 years at THS. I was in the front row too, so I had an excellent view. Never saw, never heard of. At one point I nudged the fellow next to me and asked, Have you ever seen him (pointing) before? The answer was, No. We had a large class, in the 450 range, and combined with the physically spread-out "new" THS complex, perhaps anonymity wasn't unusual. . . What are your own memories of your THS graduation? I know some of you had your ceremony at the Warner, some sang, threw hats, forgot to move the tassel, gave speeches, etc.

Responses included: "I remember the heat that night. The gym was packed. And we were the first class to toss the caps. Got hit with the point of one coming down." . . . "I remember a bunch of us agreed ahead of time to throw our caps. It had never been done before. After the Benediction and in the seconds before the Recessional started, there was a very brief pause. No one wanted to be first. Then from the center of the student body came a 'Yahoo!' Turns out it was Eddie Litke, though I didn't know it at the time. He threw his hat maybe 3-4 feet into the air. That was all it took. Suddenly the air was filled with hats and yelling. I was later told that the announcer on WTOR, which was broadcasting the ceremony, said something about 'that wild Class Of 1966.' We marched out. The final thing we did was turn in our caps and gowns. They were being collected in a small office in A Building. Teacher Dave Bennett took my gown and asked where my cap was. I hadn't thought about it, but told him off-handedly that I threw it and I guessed it was back in the gym. He told me I had to go back and get it. Without thinking, I waved my diploma, said I was done with THS, and that if he wanted the cap, he'd have to go get it himself. Fresh, I know, and years later I apologized." . . . "How could I forget graduation. I had broken my nose playing Legion ball a few weeks prior, and surgery was required to fix it. The packing was removed that morning so I had a double dose of joy. I was somewhat dizzy, but that was normal for me in my teens." . . . "Melvina Drucker started her speech, 'On a night such as this, at the turn of the century, a young Polish girl (Madame Curie) is known to have observed -' Amazing what we remember, and why." . . . "I remember we attempted to sing our 'class song' which was written by Peggy Murack and Lorraine Allyn. But, as I recall, few knew it because we'd had our graduation rehearsals cancelled for not taking them seriously and horsing around. Needless to say, our singing of that particular song was pathetic." . . . "I remember poor Mr Wheeler. (Right, David Wheeler in the 1960s.) He tried so hard to teach us that class song." . . . "We were a huge class. I still have the article from the newspaper about our graduation glued in the back of my yearbook." . . . "Some of the best years of my life were spent at THS! Made so many lasting friendships. Grad-

uation was a very special event as I got to sing with the double octet during the ceremony." . . . "Just before I left the house on Alvord Street with my parents, I hooked the reel-to-reel tape recorder up to the radio and began recording the graduation exercises that were broadcast on WTOR (later WSNG). Graduation took place at the high school, not the Warner. I don't recall a guest speaker, but I'm sure there was one. I remember accepting my diploma from the hands of Mr. Williamson. Oh, and we sang 'Climb Every Mountain,' of course. Following the ceremony I wrote this: 'Oh yes, I graduated. I squeaked by. The ceremony was dreadfully boring, and oh, so uselessly solemn! The processional, the invocation, the salute to the flag, the dull trite salutatories, recitations, and valedictories, and the endless string of awards and harangues about The Future Before You Now, and the minute-long pauses for no apparent reason, and the recessional. Only four things saved it: 1. the music, 2. the presentation of diplomas, 3. the kid behind me making the wise cracks, and 4. the moment it was through." . . . "Not much went on. If I recall, it was in the HS gym, it was very hot, and we had only 2 tickets which meant my mother and then girl friend (and now wife)

(Above, a ticket for the Class Of 1967's graduation. Tickets could be hard to come by, outside the allotted two, due to the large class sizes.)

got to sit in the bleachers while my father had to stand outside. I do remember Charlie Duggan shaking my hand while saying, 'You made it' with an almost disbelief look on his face. I spent a lot of time in detention where I learned what a great guy he was." . . . "Sadly, don't recall that graduation was a particularly memorable event. However, I do recall the practices with Mr. Wheeler for 'You'll Never Walk Alone,' and the wording emphasis on holding your 'head dup pie.' At least that is how I recall it." . . . "We wanted

to sing 'Climb Every Mountain' but they, the teachers, had other ideas. I remember during one rehearsal we tried to sing the song and we were stopped and told it wasn't the year for climbing anything, and so we sang the song they chose for us.   The teachers were not too happy with us for   trying to push for what we wanted." . . .
"Damn teachers. In those days they had the mistaken notion that graduation was about everything BUT the students. Some still hold that opinion today." . . . "Our class had a great class night at Fish & Game. So good, that naturally the TPD raided it. As the students fled the scene, one totaled his car going down the Goshen Road. Yeah, there was drinking in- volved." (Right, a large 29x36" tin sign, burnt orange in color, and signed "A.F. Tuttle

1932") . . . "Class of 1960 graduated from the Warner. Not sure how many actually crossed the stage, but there are 382 graduates (plus one memorial) listed in the yearbook. There were the usual speeches, none of which I can recall, and there were a lot of musical selections. Mr. Wheeler was busy that night. To be truthful, I cannot even remember what we did after - could not have been too exciting." . . . "I remember on class night we were going to a keg party on University Drive. But when Mr. Williamson sent home a letter to parents the day before, we chickened out. What fools; we missed out on all the fun!". . . " I remember there was a graduation party with many classmates from 1965. Cinda Gerard's parents were gracious enough to throw the party, and I attended with Rich Bognar and Mike Carrigan. Somehow earlier that night we must have been 'over served' at the Tally-Ho or someplace similar and were a bit, uh tipsy, yeah that's it. Her mom fed us coffee until we were cognizant of our surroundings and left for home. Great time." . . . "The Tally-Ho - my buddy and I started for it late afternoon pre-graduation night thinking we could make it. But we decided somewhere west of Goshen that we couldn't and turned around. One of the few times we did anything that made sense, i.e. even with the turn around we got to the high school just as the procession was about to start in." . . . "Class night was much more memorable than graduation, with a huge select party up at a West Hill cottage. Graduation kind of felt anti-climatic It was hot and in the THS gym." . . . "In 1967 I remember that those of us in the band put down our instruments halfway through 'Pomp and Circumstance' and joined the rest of the class walking out. I know that Peggy Demos and Mary Ann Tomas were the speakers. And I know there was a party for relatives at our house afterward, because there are some photos somewhere, and that's about it for

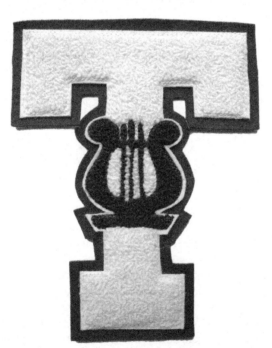

graduation. I remember Class Night a week earlier was a bit better. There was a party at John Dohanyos' cottage at West Hill. I was really pissed off that night because a friend of mine was holding hands with a girl I really liked. LOL."

(Left, a Varsity "T" for music circa 1960s, compliments of Robert "Bob" Britton.)

"I remember it was very hot in the THS gym that night. I'll always remember the song we sang. Something about 'the days of our glory was the day we were young - the days when our dreams are on parade.' It was such a pretty song that I still remember it." . . . "I remember a big party class night deep in the woods in Burrville. It was great. This was the class of 1969, which was pre-weed and predrug. Graduation night I think we partied at my friend's cottage at Tyler Lake. Ironically enough, his car got vandalized in the Farm Shop parking lot, and his house was only about 2 blocks away." . . . "Because I went to the big Class Night party stag and had a so-so time, I figured I'd get a date for after graduation. Turned out to be a smart move. One of the football players had a party at his house. I took a really good looking girl. One of those types who's so good looking the guys are afraid to ask her out. One image that stands out is our salutatorian sitting there at the party drinking a beer. I hadn't seen her outside the walls of THS in 4 years, and here she was drinking a beer like she'd been a party-goer all her life. Amazing. I heard in college she got radicalized and joined the SDS. Back to the party. It was in the finished basement. There was a closet under the stairs and lots of space behind the hanging clothes. My date and I pushed through the coats and clothes and spent most of the night in there making out, as we used to call it. The party at one point got raided by the police, but we were going at it so hot-and-heavy we didn't even know that the cops ended the party! When we finally emerged sometime around midnight, our sober-faced host was cleaning up and was shocked to see us come out of the

closet. Everyone else was long gone. Funny, and a truly memorable way to kick off post-graduation life."

Caesare 'Chet' Torsiello

Founder of "Up Your Attic," owner of Torsiello's Tavern

TORRINGTON — Caesare "Chet" Torsiello, 89, peacefully passed away Thursday, June 20, 2019, at his home surrounded by his family. He was the beloved husband of Ruth (Heinze) Torsiello for 66 years.

Chet was born Sept. 6, 1929, in Torrington, son of the late Albert and Jenny (Cerruto) Torsiello. After graduating high school, he served his country with the U.S. Army. A talented athlete, one of his many duties for the four years he served was representing the U.S. on the men's softball team.

He received several commendations for his service, including the Good Conduct Medal and Occupation Medal. He received several promotions and achieved the rank of sergeant by the time of his discharge.

While in the service in Germany, Chet met the love of his life, his future wife, Ruth. They were so young, their parents were skeptical and suggested they wait a year. After three months, Chet returned to Germany, won over his future in-laws and married Ruth. They returned to Torrington to live and start a family.

Once he returned to Torrington, Chet was employed by Allied Grocers and later started Torsiello's Tavern. After he and Ruth bought their old farmhouse, they began to enjoy going to auctions and finding treasures for their new home. Chet turned this hobby into a new career, helping auctioneers and buying and selling estates.

And so "Up Your Attic" was born. For many years, Chet could be found at flea markets and auctions all over the Northwest Corner of Connecticut and beyond. He loved people and he was great at making a deal.

Next to his beloved wife, Chet loved his big family. He was always interested in hearing about each accomplishment and he was there to celebrate so many.

In addition to his wife, he is survived by three daughters, Coleen Peterson and her husband Herb, of Torrington, Sharon Cable and her husband James, of Canton, Lesley Mara and her husband Dan, of Bloomfield; seven grandchildren, Bettina Evans and her husband Eric, Wendy Peterson, Allyn Peterson and his wife Jennifer, Tom Cable, Alex Cable, Ben Mara, Kate Mara; four great-grandchildren, Emmett Evans, Samuel Evans, Riley Peterson, Naomi Peterson; as well as several nieces and nephews.

He was preceded in death by two brothers, Frank Torsiello and Anthony Torsiello, and two sisters, Catherine Milici and Florence Meyer.

Funeral services will be on Thursday, with the cortege leaving at 10:30 a.m. from Cook Funeral Home, 82 Litchfield St., Torrington, to St. Peter Church (St. John Paul the Great Parish), 99 E. Main St., Torrington, for a Mass of Christian Burial at 11 a.m. Burial will follow at Hillside Cemetery. Relatives and friends may call on Thursday morning from 9 a.m. to 10:30 a.m. at Cook Funeral Home.

Memorial contributions may be made to FOCUS Center for Autism, 126 Dowd Ave., Canton, CT 06019; or to Connecticut Children's Medical Center, 282 Washington St., Hartford, CT 06106.

Condolences may be sent to the Torsiello family by visiting cookfuneralhomect.com.

Post: "Chet" Torsiello

If you were a tavern goer back-in-the-day, you might have hit Torsiello's which was on East Albert Street, roughly across from Doyle's, which itself was on the intersection of South Main and East Albert. Sad to report that the owner, Chet Torsiello (THS Class Of 1947), recently passed. On the left is his obituary. Chet was a friendly guy who made a very conservative, but very popular meatball grinder. He'd cut a grinder roll in half, put one meatball on each half, then proceed to cut them razor thin, spread them out, add cheese, peppers, sauce and serve 'em up with a smile. VERY tasty. Chet led an active life and leaves a townful of people with happy memories of him. RIP Chet Torsiello.

Responses included: " I remember that huge jar of pickled eggs behind the bar." . . . "Pickled eggs - standard Torrington tavern fare. And boy! did those pickled eggs taste lousy. Guess you'd have to be pretty loaded to enjoy them. The only worse food was the pickled pigs knuckles. I tried one once. Took a teeny-tiny bite. UGH!!! TOTALLY inedible. Could not swallow it. Resisted the urge to do a spit take. Don't know how those old timers ate that gristled sour crap." . . . "Chet was a nice man. He would buy you a beer after you bought 3." . . . "Any big football game at Fuessenich, such as Naugy and Ansonia, got us males headed to Chet's at halftime. No memory of a female ever being in there, i.e. that's just the way the old tavern scene was, with a few exceptions." . . . "Chet had the kielbasa and sauerkraut in a crock for days!" . . . "But he washed that crock pot only occasionally. When I opened my own tavern, he sent me a flower arrangement." . . . "I remember back when 3 members of the police force played cards there regularly. There were Mike (Gonk), Bob Neidt, and Ugo. This was shortly before Ugo died playing softball." . . . "We would always start our Friday/Saturday nights at Torsiello's around 6:30. Chet was just a good sort, and we all loved him. A few drafts, a game of pool and the bowling machine, and off we went. I had a clamming permit in those days and went to Watch Hill on the bay side. I'd always bring clams back for Chet and some of his regulars. Mr. Chaberak was always there at the tavern and was the coach of the South End Spiders. He was always challenging local neighborhoods to a football game. PS: A lot of people missed the 3rd quarter of the annual Thanksgiving football game against Watertown because of Chet's bar."

(Right, Chet Torsiello as he appeared in his 1947 THS yearbook photo.)

45

Post: Delivering The Newspaper

Presenting today a couple of vintage newspaper canvas bags. These weren't regular tote bags but were heavy-duty and used by the carrier back when newspaper delivery people were pre-teens or teens who walked or rode a bike. These bags were almost always large enough to fit all the papers, exception being the Sunday edition of the Waterbury *Republican-American*. . . Anyone here a former paperboy/papergirl? There was pretty good money in it, and it sure beat mowing lawns or shoveling snow.

Responses included: "I used to do my friends' routes when they were on vacation or sick. Doubt that many kids would want to do it today, although the tips and the occasional cookies were very good." . . .
"My brother David and I shared a route (as we called it) on Roosevelt, Funston, and a bit of High Street. And I do remember it being lucrative!" . . . "I delivered *TV Guide*, not newspapers. Less money, but less work too. They were 15 cents each and came out weekly. I made only 4 cents per magazine and relied on tips. I had 11 customers at one time, all within a mile of my house. Forty-four cents a week wasn't much, even in 1958, but it kept me off the - er, no, not off the streets, but out of trouble. And at Christmas time I made three or four bucks a week in tips. Eventually I got tired of it, and my sister took over." . . . "I have two of those newspaper bags

which are in terrible shape. I've used them to pick corn in for many years. Perfect size and sturdy." . . . "In 1966-'67 I delivered the Waterbury *Republican* by bicycle to several homes from Wyoming Avenue to Felicity Lane - up Litchfield St from the hospital. I don't remember what I did in the winter when there was too much snow to bike. I must have walked. I passed the route on to my brother when I started baby sitting. Baby sitting at 50 cents per hour was more lucrative - and did not require getting up early!" . . . "I believe that's the same route my brother had delivering *The Torrington Register* in the early '60s. I would cover the route for him when he was at Scout Camp. I recall he let me keep the 'tips.' " . . . "I delivered both newspapers: Waterbury *Republican* in the North End and *The Torrington Register* just east of Main Street and Pearl." . . . "I delivered the Waterbury *Republican* along Litchfield Street and some side streets in the early 1960s. Weekdays were fine, but the weekend papers were huge!" . . . "My son delivered *The Torrington Register* to the senior housing on Torringford West. Great experience! Most of the residents cherished all of the delivery people and traded them like long lost company. It did become challenging during the hot summer days when customers would insist that he take an ice cream to eat along the way. Because he couldn't bear to disappoint his customers, his mom (me) washed that *dripping* canvas quite often." . . . "Ahhh, your son had a primo route. All those deliveries were in one location. There was another route that was a prized route. In that one a large number of *Torrington Registers* was left at the guard shack at the Torrington Company. Now how the 'paperperson' got paid was another thing." . . . "I had the enjoyment of having and using both bags. Great experience, especially when one wanted to add on to his route by buying a customer or a route from some other paper boy." . . . "I had a *Register* route that covered a few blocks in the North End. The paper cost 42 cents a week. Most people would give me a 50 cent piece for the tip. I was so glad that *The Register* came in the afternoon at that time. No way I would have delivered a morning paper." . . . "My kids had a route. When it was bad weather, I would drive them. When The Register Company decided to go to a morning route, guess who took my bike with saddle bags on it and delivered - me! I made out pretty good because of the one-on-one contact (adult to adult), plus I always put the papers where they never got wet." . . . "I had a West End route with the Waterbury *Republican* I cleared 3 dollars a week. Got bit by a dog once. The mutt tore my trousers, and there was blood all over. Mom treated it and that was it. Not many lawyers back then." . . . "I delivered newspapers on Highland Lake by boat. My partner had the boat. He drove, and I ran from dock-to-dock." . . . "I delivered on the Red Mountain. Avenue and North Elm area." . . .

"I think I may have been the one of the first paper 'girls.' Probably started around 1958-'59. I delivered *The Register* in the West End. I picked up the papers at the corner of Central and Chestnut Avenues, which was Al's Garage at the time. My route covered Central Avenue, from Chestnut to Maplewood, Maplewood from Central to Highland. Then Smith Street, and Highland Avenue from Smith Street to the bottom. I delivered in all kinds of weather, by foot or by bike. Sometimes I even used a sled. Brings back great memories." . . . "In the late 1950s I'd see an attractive young girl picking up *The Torrington Register* at the corner of Wadhams and Main. She delivered in that area. I don't remember her name." . . . "I had a *Torrington Register* route for Amherst and Dartmouth streets. Easy work, easy money!" . . . "Every year at Christmas The Register company gave you a new bag and a $5 bill. Back in the mid-60s you didn't make much. A soda was a dime, a candy bar was a nickel. You could have fun with what you made." . . . "Once in a while I accompanied Ray Turri on his route." . . . "I had a Waterbury *Republican* route in 1960-'61. It was the biggest *Republican* route in town, slightly over 60 customers. I got the route from Jim

Mazzarelli. He'd really built it into a monster, i.e. many customers, and a lengthy walk. Jim was 3 years older, and he could carry the newspapers himself everyday. Me, I could do it everyday but Sunday. Then the papers wouldn't even fit into 2 bags. On Sunday my father would drop half the bundle off at Walnut Street, the halfway mark. On days like Thursday the bag would be packed tight, a big heavy perfect rectangle with the newspapers that didn't fit in tucked under my arm. The newspaper bundle was dropped off at the intersection of Albert and New Litchfield, around where Burger Chef was. Then I'd walk up New Litchfield, do the side streets like Earle and Broad, go up Walnut to Hillside Cemetery, come back down, do McKinley top-to-bottom, then Belleview, Travis, and Blake Street. I'd be on the papers at 5:30 a.m. and finish around 7. Thursday around supper time I'd walk, sometimes ride my bike, over the route again collecting. Some people left the money out, but mostly I had to knock on the door. One guy, who was always drunk, would ask me how much he owed, and would always say, *That* much? Then he'd usually tell me that he'd catch me next week. It usually took 3-4 weeks for him to finally pay up. Tips were great! One guy alone gave me $1 every week as long, as he said, he   had his newspaper before 6 a.m., which he always did because he was near the beginning of the route. I was clearing $13-14 a week, which was big money for a 12/13-year-old. Sundaes back then were 50¢, and I enjoyed an occasional one at Doyle's and Opperman's. But mostly I saved my earnings. Saved enough to buy a motorcycle when I was in college, but that's another story. I eventually gave up the route when I just got tired of getting up so early. Made for a very long day."

(Right, an old illustration of the Water Street building when it was built in 1881.)

Post: Learning To Swim At The Torrington YMCA

Who remembers swim classes in the old YMCA 20-yard pool? Below are 2 different stages regarding that. The first is undated but is probably from the 1920s. This boys swim class occurred at a time when males frequented the pool in the buff, which I believe is the case with this class. . . The second picture (p.52) is a swim class in the old pool from the mid-1960s. This is more how I remember it being when I joined during "Learn To Swim Week" in 1953. . . What are your own memories of learning to swim and/or dive at the Torrington YMCA?

(Above, the old Y 20-yard pool circa 1920s. By the 1960s all of these windows and radiators would be gone, the ceiling would be lowered, and the benches taken out. The tile work, to include the pattern and "3½ FEET DEEP," as well as the metal lion head whose mouth actually hid the water pipe for adding water, are all still in place today in the 21st century.)

Responses included: "Renny Belli was my swim instructor, when I was six or so. And yes, it was in the buff. For that matter, so was Phys Ed swimming at the old high school with Coach Bonetti around 1956." . . . "I enjoyed the classes in the early 1960s and rose to

Flying Fish. Had a tough instructor named Rudy." . . . "Rudy Valenzi from Beverly, Massachusetts. Wonderful person, but very intimidating due to his height and large physique. When he told a non-swimmer to try this, try that, there was no way the kid wouldn't." . . . "I taught at the Y for years. Loved every minute of it. And I remember being so proud to have passed Shark at age 9! They didn't have Porpoise yet. Spent many wonderful hours there." . . .

(Below, a Shark Test card from the Torrington Y, 1960s. The original is pale yellow in color.)

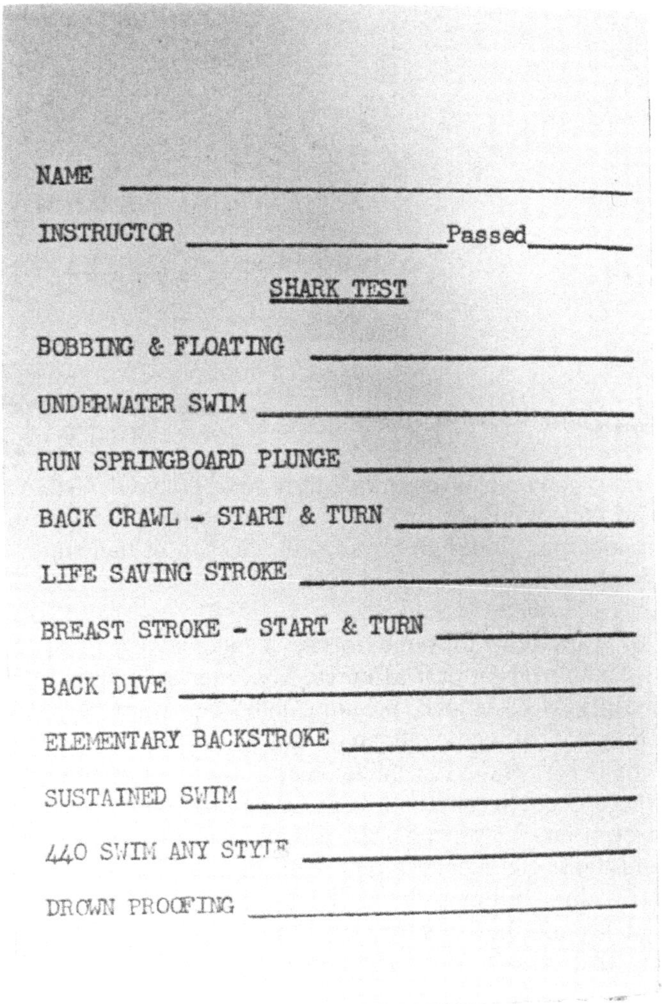

NAME _____

INSTRUCTOR _____ Passed_____

SHARK TEST

BOBBING & FLOATING _____

UNDERWATER SWIM _____

RUN SPRINGBOARD PLUNGE _____

BACK CRAWL – START & TURN _____

LIFE SAVING STROKE _____

BREAST STROKE – START & TURN _____

BACK DIVE _____

ELEMENTARY BACKSTROKE _____

SUSTAINED SWIM _____

440 SWIM ANY STYLE _____

DROWN PROOFING _____

. . . "I loved the learn-to-swim cards. Different colors for each level. A checklist of skills to learn. They got wet and wrinkled. It was pure motivation." . . . "I fondly remember taking classes at the Y and enjoyed all of them as a kiddo. Great experience." . . . "I still have my Flying Fish award. Great memories." . . .

(Above, a boys swim class in the shallow end of the old YMCA pool, 1960s. The non-swimmers in the water are holding onto the gutter practicing kicking, while the boys on the deck wait their turn. Note that the windows are now bricked over.)

"I tried to learn how to swim in the Y pool at age 7-8, around 1957-'58, and never got past Minnow. My sister brought me to West Hill, and Billy Mills helped me jump into deep water and not die. Saw the future. That whole: 'I can do this thing.' Years later (1964) I returned to the Y pool. Freshman year - slow. Sophomore year - breakthrough. Pool became one of the most important places for me, then and even now. Twenty yards, low ceiling, narrow seating area for visitors, fans, etc. Coach Evers. Bill, Paul, Frank, Chris G., Bill John (RIP), Jim Rubino, Doug Traub, others. Weeknights we'd practice at 8 p.m. We'd get word upstairs, while we were playing ping pong that it was time, and run down that circular staircase.

Reminded me of something out of Hard Days Night." . . . "I always thought this was a big pool as a little lad." . . . "Ah, great memories. Robert Kelly taught us in the early 1950s. He went on to become a principal at North School then at East School. He used to reminisce about his early YMCA days." . . . "I learned to swim at the Y and later became an instructor in the Learn-To-Swim program. I remember the joy when a kid finally passed swimming the length of the pool. That was the Frank Gillis-Ken Barton era. GREAT MEMS!" . . . "Polywog, Minnow, Fish, Flying Fish, Shark. I can still smell the chlorine. Renny Belli taught me how to do a back dive. I did it poorly. My chin met the board, and 6 stitches later I decided back diving was not for me!" . . . "I was also a part of the swim program for years. Loved it. Still remember seeing rainbows around the lights. The chlorine was particularly bad. No goggles in those days. Can't believe they allowed swimming in the buff back then." . . . "I loved diving. Today, that seems unbelievably scary to me." . . . "I remember being so excited going through the ranks from Polywog to Shark! Good times."

(Above, the original Torrington YMCA on Main Street, which today is the antiques store and restaurant Remember When. Photo is circa late 1890s/ early 1900s. This Y had no pool, and only a very small gymnasium. Note the 3 young men in front proudly posing with their bicycles, which are in a bike rack. Note also the beautiful large elm trees which lined Main before the Dutch Elm Disease wiped them out.)

Post: The Hendey Machine Company

In its day (1870-1954), The Hendey Machine Company was said to manufacture the best machine tools in the world. To orient the reader to where exactly Hendey was (its official address was 105-123 Summer Street), I've included a picture of its front gate (below) and a map of the plant layout (opposite page). The front gate sat right across from TV Lab today - at the intersection of Litchfield and New Litchfield Streets and Turner Avenue. . . Hendey Machine Company was founded in Wolcottville, now the downtown area of Torrington, in 1870. Henry J. Hendey was a machinist, and he founded the business with the idea that machines built to very exacting precision would always find a market. He partnered with his brother Arthur, and together they began operations in a small, one-story building on New Litchfield Street. Two years later they built a 40x60' building on the site of what-was-to-be the later complex, and from there business took off. Product lines slowly expanded, sales went worldwide, and always there was attention to precision and detail. Sadly, Hendey's sold in 1954, and the manufacturing ceased. Part of the plant eventually became Charter Oak, which lasted a number of years.

(Above, the front gate of the old Hendey's, circa 1942-'43.)

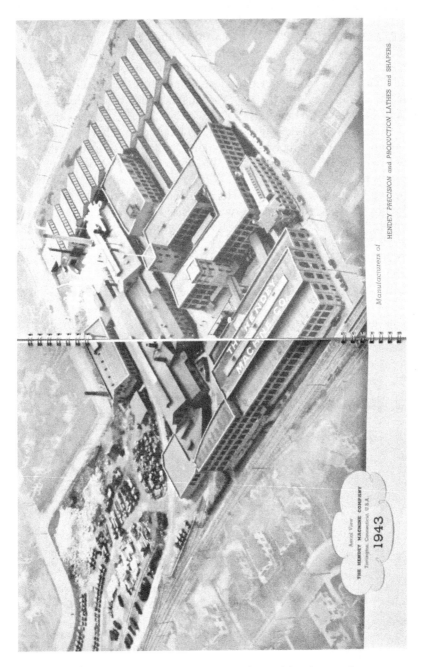

(Above, the plant layout [rotate the page]. The parking lot can be seen on the left. Running alongside the right of the plant is Summer Street.)

Responses included: "My dad worked there, from THS graduation in 1935 until he enlisted for the war in 1942." . . . "There is a Hendey lathe in the Smithsonian Arts and Industries Museum." . . . "I worked at Charter Oak Container Corp., making corrugated cardboard boxes in the summer of 1967." . . . "Top quality machines, reflected in the very high quality literature. I enjoyed seeing the traffic directional sign (first picture) near the front gate. Don't remember seeing that in my uncountable walks past that spot. Our family moved to that part of town in 1952, when I was 10. Walking or biking to downtown was pretty routine, as I recall." . . . "Of course you were walking past it before I was. My walks past Hendey started in 1955, the year of the Flood, the year after Hendey went under. I don't remember that sign either. But it sure is pretty neat." . . . "My grandfather was a foreman at Hendey's. When we bought our farmhouse in Pennsylvania in the 1970s we found a Hendey lathe in one of the outbuildings! The previous owner showed up one day and asked if he could take the lathe (he had forgotten about it when he moved out, apparently). That was OK with us. I told him about my grandfather. He said, 'Maybe your grandfather participated in making this lathe.' Maybe he did."

(Above, 1943. Former foreman and 50-year-man Daniel Cameron on the left enjoys visiting with the current work force and sharing a laugh.)

. . . "My dad worked at Hendey's until they closed. He started as an apprentice after WWII and worked there until they closed." . . . "My father worked there too. I'm not sure if he apprenticed there or elsewhere. Somewhere I have a letter from the company to my grandfather congratulating him on the apprenticeship of his son. They don't do that sort of thing any more. Too bad."

(Above, a view of the planing, heavy milling, and boring floor. This area is where the main castings from the foundry of Hendey's went to be shaped.)

(Above, 1943. Female office workers in Hendey's IBM Tabulating Room, "where all card records are mechanically converted into operating costs and payroll calculations.")

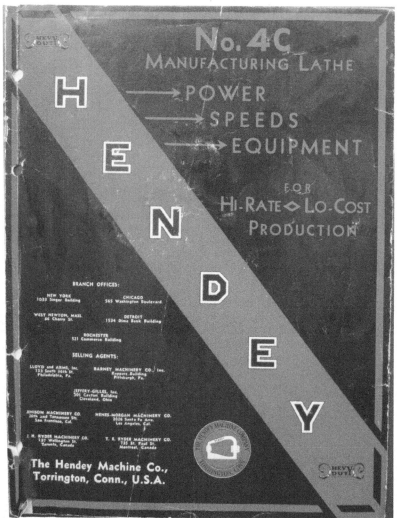

(Above, the cover of an undated sales booklet. Note the 4 perforations along the spine, i.e. this booklet was undoubtedly kept in a loose-leaf binder for reference. The left side cites 5 branch offices: New York in the Singer Building, Chicago, Detroit, Rochester, and West Newton, MA. Selling agents are also cited and are located in Philadelphia, Pittsburgh, Cleveland, San Francisco, Los Angeles, Toronto, and Montreal. . . Booklet compliments of Jim Wright of Wright's Barn and Flea Market.)

(Above the former main gate of Hendey's in 2019. Compare this to the 1943 photo on p.54. The property is sadly abandoned, overgrown, and for sale. . . Below, the Summer Street, main office side of the complex. It's gated and mostly boarded up in 2019.)

Post: Rosie The Riveter, i.e. Torrington's Female Factory Workers

We've all heard the phrase "Rosie the Riveter" that was given to women who worked in the factories during WWII. Torrington's success as a manufacturing center was due in no small part to such women, i.e. our female labor force. From teens and young women to much older senior ladies, from office jobs in the factories to being on the plant floor, generations of Torrington ladies did more than their fair share of helping our manufacturers succeed. Did you have any female family members who worked in our myriad of manufacturing plants: The Torrington Company, Torin, Hendey's, Fitzgerald, Turner & Seymour, Haydon Manufacturing Company, Torrington Casting, Warrenton Woolen Mill, Union Hardware, The Progressive Manufacturing Company, et al.? My mother-in-law, Helen Perzanowski, worked in Fitzgerald's for years. It was an easy walk from the family home on Newfield Road to Fitzie's. . . Did you yourself (ladies only) work in industry? Please share any memories you have of our own "Rosie the Riveters."

(Above, Torrington women operating high-speed drills in Hendey, WWII.)

Responses included: "My mother, Marion Hurlbut, worked in the Accounting Office at the Torrington Company for years. She worked after graduating THS in 1939 until after she and Dad married in '45." . . . "During the war my Mom worked for the Torrington Company. She and my Dad did not get married until after the war because he didn't want to leave her a widow. Once they married in 1946 my Mom stopped working and never worked again."

(Above, female workers at Excelsior, a.k.a. The Needle Shop, circa 1920s. Females long before WWII had become an invaluable part of the work force in Torrington. . . From Torrington Company literature regarding the WWI period: "At the time it was felt that female employees were especially fastidious with hand work. Thus, when it came to making surgical needles, it was decided that about 90% of the work force should be comprised of women and girls." The Torrington Company actively recruited new female personnel both from within Torrington and from neighboring towns. With transportation for commuting a problem in those long ago days, the Torrington Company needed to find a place where new, out-of-town female workers could live, sleep, and eat. In 1917 the company bought the Conley Inn, a.k.a. The Yankee Pedlar, downtown and converted it to a female "dormitory." After WWI it was converted back to a hotel, but females and factory work in Torrington were now inextricable linked.)

. . . "I worked summers at the Turner & Seymour, 1968-'70. My mother worked there full time as well, as many women did. One of the first things I noticed was the women operating the huge presses had cuffs around their wrists that pulled their arms back when the machine was hit (pressed). I asked one of the ladies "why" the wrist cuffs, and she showed me her hands. She only had 6 fingers left and four nubs. Injuries were common, and I still have a scar on my thumb which was almost cut off. The head of Human Resources, who was also the medic, taped me up and sent me back to work. Then, there was the foundry. . ." . . . "My Mom and Dad were both basically factory lifers. Mom was at the Torrington Company, and she inspected parts, mostly bearings I believe."

(Above, women in the Torrington Company's Broad Street Plant inspect needle rollers, circa 1960s.)

. . . "My sister worked at the Torrington Co. for about 40 years packing ball bearings. Her husband also worked there." . . . "I did one college summer at the Standard Plant. Extremely educational experience, and what I noted then, and still remember, was the number of women working the machines, both large and small. Evidently, the trend carried right into the sixties." . . . "My grandmother worked at the Torrington Company. We lived on Pythian Avenue, and she walked to-and-from work. She also took her own lunch and used the same brown bag for days on end!" . . . "Both

my Mom and Aunt worked for the Torrington
Company (Needle Division). My Mom got a
needle caught in one of her thumb nails, and
ever since then, her nail grew in with ridges
in it." . . . "Several of my aunts worked at the
Excelsior and Standard plants during that
time." . . .

(Right, a small brass and enamel case for
carrying needles. Compliments of the Robert
Britton collection.)

. . . "My Mom worked at Fitzgerald's. All my
mother ever said was she worked in the
gasket mill, and my grandmother never said
anything. My grandmother worked at Torin.
She retired at 65, the next year her friends
threw her a 75th birthday party. Guess she lied
about her age to keep working. This was
before Social Security. I do know after retiring
my grandmother took care of the rooms for the
men living at the Elks Club to earn a bit." . . . "My
mom and one aunt worked for Torin. Another aunt worked at Fitzie's.
And the third aunt was at the Torrington Company." . . . "After my
grandmother lost her husband at age 40, she had to work to support
two children and was employed by Fitzgerald's, operating a machine
to which her arms were strapped, so they would be pulled back
automatically and not injured by the machine. According to the
adage, 'What doesn't kill you, makes you stronger.' My grandmother
lived to be 100!" . . . "My Mom worked at the Torrington Company
for over 30 years. She worked on some kind of press that was very
dangerous. She had a few of her fellow workers lose a finger or
two." . . . "I worked at Sun Chief factory in Winsted one summer
during college. They had an assembly line opened up just for the
summer for students. We mostly made rotisserie ovens. I put the
motors in! Whenever people were absent from the main lines, they
would move some of us to that line to fill in. I did it several times—
put guide wires into toasters. I got a ride with a girl from Litchfield
named Mara. I walked down to the corner of New Litchfield and
Walnut Streets every morning for 6 a.m. pick up. Decided that would
not be my lifelong career!" . . . "Many of my female THS classmates
worked during the summer of 1967 on an assembly line at Waring in

New Hartford. I carpooled with one of them. I sat all day long using an electric screwdriver to attach metal plates to the bottoms of blender bases. Management really pushed us hard some days because they could, and they knew we weren't coming back! The company played 3 or 4 tunes repeatedly all summer. If I ever hear 'MacArthur's Park' again. . ." . . . "My aunt worked at the Torrington Company, Needle Division and my grandmother worked at Turner and Seymour, making kitchen stuff." . . . "My first job after high school was at the Excelsior Plant of the Torrington Company. I put sewing machine needles - merrow and blindstitch - into a projector

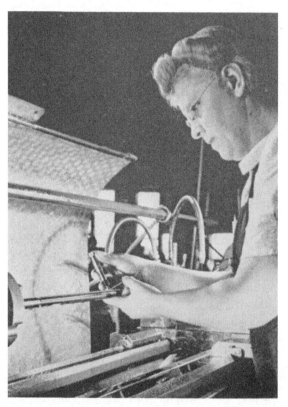

and adjusted them to specific tolerances. The job paid $1.87½ cents an hour, plus piecework. I loved it. Because of this, I was able to join the National Society of Descendants of Textile Workers of America."

(Left, a female supervisor in Hendey during WWII checking the thread diameter of a cross-feed screw.)

. . . "I worked at Torin one summer when I was in college. I did spot (arc) welding. When I got hired, the guy who hired me thought I would maybe last a week. I lasted the whole summer with plenty of burn holes in my shirts (back in the day when you had to wear skirts to work as well)."
. . . "My Grandma worked at Hayden's. I was very fortunate to be able to work at Fitzgerald's while going to St. Joe's College. They

were great to me, and I met many wonderful people there. Best of all, I learned what a 'gasket' was. I was one of the first women there to wear slacks. I remember sitting in the Ladies Room, a.k.a. The Break Room, when the other ladies told me that slacks were not allowed.". . . "We live in Marathon, Florida, now and I had the privilege to meet the real Rosie the Riveter. She was quite a character."

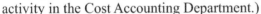

(Above & below, a few of the female workers at Hendey circa 1940s. Above, women file and remove burrs on transmission gears. Below, activity in the Cost Accounting Department.)

Post: SLOW DOWN! - Danger On Our City Streets

Mother-of god, (some) people, SLOW DOWN! or you will surely kill someone. . . I must have a target on my back, or rather a bullseye plastered all over my Hyundai Tucson. Yesterday I'm stopped at a stop sign at the intersection of Park Avenue and East Albert, Senior Center parking lot to my right. I look both ways, double check, then ease forward about to take a right. A lady in a red SUV runs the stop sign to my left. She's heading east towards Route 8 and is really FLYING. Thank heavens my peripheral vision still works. I slam on the brakes, stop dead, and lay on the horn. She rockets by, then hits her own brakes probably realizing what she had just done, and *almost* just done. She reduces her speed to the 25 limit, with hopefully a valuable lesson learned, i.e. the red octagon sign with white letters means STOP! . . . The other driver today was NOT so lucky. About an hour ago I'm heading south on Franklin Street just past the old Trip's Variety Store (almost visible on the left in the picture on the opposite page). I'm moseying along as per my retiree, no-rush ways, and a white pickup truck comes screaming around the slight bend in the street. The male driver is ON MY SIDE OF THE ROAD! and must be going 60 MPH, a.k.a. a real bat-out-of-hell. Again I lay on the horn, pull over as much as I can, and in the nanosecond I see him as he swerves by, I can see a look of astonishment on his face. He makes it mostly back into his lane, but is going SO fast he loses control. He slams into a parked car (opposite picture) and hits it so hard he pushes it onto the sidewalk where it upends a trash container. I pull over and stop. He pulls over and stops. The impact is so loud, neighbors are now running out of their houses. No one's in the parked car, thank god. Driver and passenger in the pickup both OK. Glass and debris all over the street as if a garbage truck just upended. I call 911, give my contact info and oral report, and am told I can leave. As I get back into my car, one of the onlookers says to me, There are lots of kids in this neighborhood. He shakes his head and asks rhetorically, Why would anyone be driving that fast? It's a good question, and I have no answer. I DO know that the 40ish male driver in the pickup was damn lucky he didn't kill anyone, to include me. . .

Responses included: "One day you write about cars going too slow, another day you write about one going too fast." . . . "Probably a morning drinker." . . . "Never would have happened if that driver had

had Mr. Faita (the old Torrington driving instructor) as an instructor."
. . . "True. We drove better in the old days." . . . "You people must
have dementia! The old days were NOT so great. Remember the
teens peeling out, speeding, and drag racing! I don't know how many
tickets the TPD handed out in the 1960s to teens and young folk, but
we sure kept them busy!". . . Wonder if he was on a cell phone, or
drugs?" . . . "Bet he didn't learn a thing. It'll probably happen again."
. . . "Torrington isn't the town it used to be. Too many distracted
drivers, both young and old. Too many speeders too. School signs,
speed limit signs, construction zone signs - none of them mean a
thing to many. The Torrington Police Department really needs to
crack down. They should be conducting more spot checks and setting
up more radar." . . . "Isn't there a tavern and a package store near
here? I'm not saying they're connected with the accident, but it's
possible." . . . "You sure were lucky Bentley that you're not dead.
You must live a good, clean life. LOL"

(Above, Franklin Street looking north towards East Main with the accident
scene on the right. Note how the passenger car has been pushed up onto the
sidewalk and lawn. An upended trash receptacle is in front of the
demolished car.)

Post: Catherine Calhoun - An Accomplished Woman

Catherine Clarissa Calhoun, August 3, 1903 - May 16, 1986. She was the librarian at THS for 37 years: 1930-'67. She once told the story of how she got the job. "Superintendent George Vogel called me one day and said, 'I need a high school librarian, and you're it.' I said, 'Who says?' and he said, 'I say. Come down tomorrow morning and we'll talk about it.' " Catherine Calhoun, who eventually became known as "Cagey" went on to a long career at THS. She herself had graduated the Church Street school in 1921, i.e. 9 years before she went back as a faculty member. In the intervening years she'd graduated from Connecticut College, did graduate work at Yale, and worked for the state Welfare Department and the Torrington Library. Below, is a picture of her sitting with part of her graduating THS class. Which one is she? She's in the front row, dead center, a very

attractive teen. She was a well known member of her class, serving on The Tabula (school newspaper) staff and ultimately being voted "Most Dignified" in the class superlatives. She DOES look dignified, and certainly always WAS her own woman. She lived most, if not all, of her life on Cook Street, a great central location. In her youth the Park Theatre was steps away on the corner of South Main & Cook. I have no doubt that the very literate and imaginative young Catherine spent many hours in that theatre. In later years she could walk to THS and probably often did. It's reported that although she could and did drive, in her retirement years as the director of the Historical Society, she walked. The only thing that might support the notion that she drove a *lot* at one time is that fact that in the summer of 1934 she and her good friend Dorothea Cramer (THS Class Of 1920 and the head Torrington librarian) went on a cross country trip to Yellowstone, Salt Lake, and many other points of interest. They covered 5477 miles in an old Model T that they christened "The Darling Child." It seems unlikely that Dorothea would have done all of that driving. . .

(Above, Dorothea Cramer at the circulation desk of The Torrington Library in April 1973 when she was close to retirement. She's checking out a book for 10-year-old Teddy Nowakowski.)

. . . Catherine Clarissa Calhoun's career didn't end with her THS retirement. As befitting a strong, single woman she served on numerous boards, a.k.a. she was president of the Northwest Girl Scout Council, vice chairperson of the American Red Cross, regent of the Marana Brooks Chapter of of the DAR, clerk of the vestry of Trinity Church, et. al. In 1954 the Quota Club of Litchfield County named her Woman Of The Year. All these accomplishments, honors, and positions are surprising to those of us who only knew Catherine Calhoun during our teen years at THS. Most of us, undoubtedly, thought of her as a Ssshhhing! librarian: very strict, very disciplined. And she was that, and also the type who didn't suffer fools gladly.

The story's told how a researcher showed up at the Historical Society to use the archives. Ms. Calhoun asked him what he was researching, and when he said "trolleys in Torrington," she told him that it'd already been done, and more than once, then closed the door in his face. BUT, she was also the type of person who had a terrific memory, had seen a LOT of Torrington in the 20th century, and knew

(Below, a picture of the 11-year-old Catherine Calhoun at the THS cornerstone laying ceremony in 1914. She appears to be holding a box of some sort. Behind her is her father John, a long time school committee member. The gentleman in the forefront is Nathan A. Tuttle, a man who served on many Torrington boards and was a VIP at the Woolen Mill. The dog on the far left with its paw in the air was Tuttle's dog "Major." Photo, Collection of the Torrington Historical Society)

most everyone and most everything local. That's the Catherine Calhoun I would LOVE to talk with today. PS: I'd also have some personal questions for her, but that might take sharing a bottle, or two, of spirits.

Responses included: "I remember her well." . . . "She was referred to as 'Cagey Calhoun,' seemingly always stern, but very helpful. Would have been great to know her outside of THS years later." . . .

"She ran a tight ship in that library, but yes, she was really there to help. For her, it was all about the students." . . . "All through high school and even all through college, I had no idea what I wanted to be, but I'm sure that in my wildest imagination I never thought of Librarian. It turned out to be a great career though (and way different from that of Miss Calhoun and Miss Cramer at the Torrington Library, not that I'm being critical of them)." . . . "What we liked to do in the library was 'set' shelves, i.e. you would pull out the supporting pins allllllmost all the way, then sit back and wait. Invariably some unsuspecting under-classmen would come along, take a book from that shelf, and the shelf would come crashing down, books flying. It was highly amusing and entertaining, especially watching Cagey leap all over the puzzled and terrified 'guilty' one. Usually we'd set a shelf, forget about it, and days would pass before it crashed. We'd be as surprised as the victim when it happened." . . .

(Right, a rather stern looking Miss Calhoun in the THS library in 1966 standing alongside the somewhat new shelving. Are any of these shelves "set" to come tumbling down?. . .)

. . . "Even my parents called her Cagey Calhoun

(not disrespectfully, I believe). That must have been her nickname even outside of school. You know where that name comes from, right? Cagey Calhoun was a character in Ann Sothern's 1950's sitcom 'Private Secretary.' " . . . "Nellie Sullivan + Catherine Calhoun = women of mystery. Though Cagey was far more, what's the word? Striking? Fashionable? Charismatic? Warm/Fuzzy?" . . . "Haha. Love 'warm/fuzzy.' Actually, compared to Nellie, Catherine was Mother Theresa + June Cleaver." . . . "I remember her well, as I do Dorothea Cramer. Both gentle ladies, and outstanding librarians." . . . "Interesting background, especially the cross-country trip to Yellowstone - pretty adventurous for two women in a Model T back in 1934. I wonder if they encountered any car trouble or a flat tire and whether they were able to fix the problems themselves." . . . "Great name: Catherine Clarissa Calhoun." . . . "Such an interesting read. I only knew her as a somewhat serious women who ran the school library. It's nice to see another side!" . . . "I worked at the Torrington Library throughout high school. Dorothea Cramer was a force to be reckoned with. We were all both terrified of her and loved her!" . . .

(Above, Catherine Calhoun in the center of the picture, 1959, in the old THS library surrounded by a dozen student "assistants." Library assistants were usually (always?) female. Whether this was a written policy, or just a result of the social mores of the time, is unknown.)

. . . "Catherine Calhoun, I stayed out of her way, and she stayed out of mine. Life was easier that way." . . . "She lived across from us on Cook Street, and I think she drove and lived with her brother (John).

We all stayed away from her, although she never bothered us. We went by her nickname 'Cagey' Calhoun."

(Above, 44 Cook Street in 2019. Note the carriage house at the rear of the property. This house is where Catherine Calhoun and her family lived for most/all of Catherine's life. . . Below, Ms. Calhoun in 1961, flashing a lovely, but rarely seen, smile.)

Post: Dorothea Cramer and Katherine Calhoun - Twin Lives

We recently discussed longtime THS librarian Catherine Calhoun and in doing so touched upon Dorothea Cramer, the longtime city of Torrington librarian. A little bit of deeper delving reveals that the 2 ladies had much in common. Dorothea was born in 1902, Catherine in 1903. Both lived most of their lives locally AND centrally: Catherine at 44 Cook Street, Dorothea at 113 Pearl. These were the family homes that, I assume, both Catherine and Dorothea inherited when the parents passed. They were only a year apart at THS,

Dorothea in the Class Of 1920, Catherine in the Class Of 1921. They both worked on The Tabula (school newspaper) staff.

(Left, is a picture of them standing together for a *Tabula* staff photo in 1918. They are similarly dressed; Dorothea is on the left. Photo, Collection of the Torrington Historical Society.)

Both were well known members of their classes. Catherine was voted "Most Dignified," Dorothea was "Belle."

CLASS BEAU AND BELLE.

Distinction Awarded to Franklin Thayer and Dorothea Cramer.

The class beau of the 1920 class of Torrington high school is Franklin Thayer, according to the superlatives read at the recent exercises; and Dorothea Cramer is the class belle. The most popular boy is Fred Stull and the most popular girl, Flavia Hickey.

(Left, a news brevity that appeared in the June 11, 1920 issue of *The Torrington Evening Register*.)

After THS both matriculated to Connecticut College where they graduated a year apart. Undoubtedly they saw each other there, and probably traveled together when they came home. After college, both were working at the Torrington library in the late 1920s before Catherine went to THS. Sidebar: In responding to why she became a librarian, Dorothea Cramer told a reporter in 1973, "There wasn't much for women then: nursing, secretarial work, and teaching. I wasn't interested in nursing. I didn't want to be a secretary." And she had tried teaching (3 years in Canaan) and wasn't satisfied with that. Of course, for most Torrington women in the early 20th century, the choices of profession usually came down to 2 options: marry and become a housewife. OR, go into the factories. But Dorothea and Catherine were college grad-uates, career minded, and wanted more. . . Dorothea spent 35 years as head Torrington li-brarian from 1938-1973,

(Right, Dorothea Cramer posing in her beloved Torrington Library in 1973, the year she retired. This photo hung in the library for many years. Photo, Collection of the Torrington His-torical Society)

while Catherine spent 37 years as head THS librarian from 1930- 1967. Seemingly at odds with the stereotypical, prim 'n proper librarian image, both women had a sense of adventure, and, as was previously mentioned, loved to travel as shown by their 5477 mile, cross-country trip together in the summer of 1934.

(Above, "The Darling Child," i.e. the car that Dorothea and Katherine used in their 1934 cross country trip to points west, e.g. Fort Wayne, Dome Rock [Nebraska], Salt Lake, Logan Pass [Utah], Grand Tetons, Yellowstone, Deadwood [South Dakota], Chicago, and Niagara Falls. Photo, Collection of the Torrington Historical Society)

Both women were also very active outside the libraries. Both were in the DAR, both were members of the Historical Society, the Connecticut College Alumnae Association, the Women's College Club Of Litchfield County, et al. Admittedly not all their extracurricular groups intersected. For example, Dorothea was active in the Audubon Society, Catherine in the Girl Scouts. . . When her parents died, Dorothea Cramer inherited a cottage at Highland Lake. She loved to spend time there - did Catherine join her? - though the idea of her or Catherine water skiing, open water swimming, or SCUBA diving borders on preposterous, at least in their later years. Both ladies enjoyed reading, were highly cerebral, and I found no mention of them participating in any form of sport. I was told by one source that both ladies enjoyed a tipple or two, though it was said Dorothea held her "tipples" better than Catherine did. . . Neither lady ever married. . . Dorothea died first. She was 80-years-old when she passed in 1983. Catherine followed her 3 years later in 1986 at 82-years-old. For 2 genetically unrelated women, they shared remarkably similar lives. Parallel existences, twin journeys. One Final Thing - Confession: As I've gotten to know the ladies better in the little research I've done, I've wondered in recent days if they were also lovers. The social, religious (both ladies did attend church), and professional mores of their time would have undoubtedly precluded any "coming out," for sure. BUT, I hope they were. I hope they found comfort in each other. They certainly deserved it.

Responses included: "Beautiful story. Interesting women." . . . "Great research! Wonderful to learn so much more about these ladies, both of whom touched so many lives in Torrington over the years." . . . "I enjoyed learning more about these fine ladies! Thanks!" . . . "Thanks for all the research. There were so many notable people in Torrington. All it takes is a walk through Hillside Cemetery to see the names that were Torrington. I'm sure they all had a great story to tell in the creation of our fair city!" . . . "I still remember many of the things I learned from working at the Torrington library for Miss Cramer. Even being a high school student, I was given by her the opportunity to learn many things including cataloging books and preparing them availability for patrons. She also allowed me to host story hour for the children during the summer - which I loved doing!" . . . "I appreciate learning about these women. Undoubtedly they were way ahead of their times." . . . "I remember both women from their respective libraries. I also knew Miss Cramer (a bit) from Center Church. I wish I'd known some of this information about the two woman then - they would have been more approachable. I might have asked them about that cross country trip." . . . "A truly amazing article about 2 fine women." . . . "My mother knew them both much better than I did. And she knew Catherine well enough that she volunteered to house some out of town ushers when I got married in 1963. It was hard for me to imagine two guys in their 20s actually spending the weekend at her home, but they did and she was a wonderful hostess!" . . . "Great story, and yes, they were certainly ahead of the times." . . . "You may be right about them being more than just friends."

(Above right, 113 Pearl Street today. This is the house where Dorothea Cramer spent most of her life.)

Post: A Strange Question - Are you Jewish?

Torrington never ceases to amaze me. . . So I just start to mow the lawn yesterday afternoon, when I notice a black Nissan Altima crawling up the street and starting to pull over. As much as I don't want to turn off the lawnmower, it's clear I'm going to have to when the car rolls to a stop with faces turned towards me. Inside are two young men. Both are wearing white shirts, sporting dark beards, and the driver is wearing a flat black hat. The passenger window comes down, I turn off the lawnmower, and there's a short pause as we size each other up. I'm figuring Jehovah Witnesses since they're the only ones who ever work the neighborhood, though these fellows don't look it. Perhaps, Amish, Pennsylvania Dutch? But I live on a dead-end street that's clearly marked, so it's not a drive-through, so why would two Amish lads be on this street? The passenger window is down, and the heavier young man smiles and says, Are you

Jewish?. . . Jewish? I think. Do I look Jewish, maybe a twin to Paul Newman? Is it my Brooklyn t-shirt? I want to say, Not the last time I looked down, but I only smile and say, No. . . Do you know if there's a synagogue in this town? he asks. . . There was, I say, for a long time, but it closed. The closest one now is probably in Litchfield. . . OK, he says, thanks. They smile, and off they go. I restart the lawnmower, and naturally give them a wave when they come back a minute later having hit the dead-end. . . Retrospection: Never in my life have I been asked if I was Jewish. Actually, NEVER in my life have I been asked my ethnicity, i.e. whether I'm Rumanian, French, Irish, Italian, Russian, Polish, English, etc. etc. It's a strange question. Perhaps they were just crooks, incognito, casing the neighborhood. BUT, more likely those 2 young men felt they could best trust another Jew. Wrap Up: We live in polarized times greatly abetted by FOX News and Trump. It's a tragic state of affairs when Americans believe they can only trust likes. I sweated yesterday while cutting the grass, but I sweat more over an America that would care about my ethnicity, or where I came from. . . Peace, and good will towards all this day to include old-time Swamp Yankees like me, 19ᵗʰ and 20ᵗʰ century arrivals, and ALL the newest arrivals - legal OR illegal - with the dust still on them from the journey.

Responses included: "I'll send you a Happy Hanukkah greeting now, so I don't forget." . . . "Nice post, Paul. You can be so very gentle." . . . "An interesting perspective of these days and oh! so sad times." . . . "Excellent wrap up. I feel so many people are being nudged/herded/railroaded into behaving as they never would have before. A simple human exchange on the street is no longer simple." . . . "Thanks for keeping an eye on the neighborhood." . . . "I hope they found what they wanted, in Litchfield or elsewhere. With the hats, they might have been Orthodox, and really looking for a place of worship." . . . "Well said Paul. Polarized times indeed!" . . . "Odd story. I expected the end to be long lost friends you hadn't seen for some time goofing on you. I live on a dead end as well, and we are in a Neighborhood Watch and always vigilant for cars that don't belong. The unfortunate division that is being perpetuated daily, does not help matters. Barry McGuire's song would sure be appropriate today as well, i.e. Eve Of Destruction, social destruction. And it's so unnecessary." . . . "You had a Blues Brother's sighting. Jake and Elwood have often been confused with Orthodox Jews, a common mistake." . . . "I always enjoy your political posts. So many others are so out of sync with my beliefs that I can feel the anger rising." . . . "Your street used to be a Jewish neighborhood." . . . "Great. Great last line. (I thought the photo made you look like Van Morrison, who was not Jewish, but was raised in Kingdom Hall.)" . . . "It's because you own a modern home. Many Jewish people have wonderful taste and are neat clean and organized and live the modern way." . . . "Thank you for taking the time to share yet another priceless gem. Living in L.A., I am asked that question all the time. I am also asked if I am Armenian. It has taken me just shy of 20 years to now just nod and smile. I find the Hollywood response to be one of joy and relief, instead of disappointment. If we could just love, show welcoming and positive energy to all, and welcome the 'huddled masses yearning to be free,' wouldn't life be grand? I will not linger here. You wrapped things up quite nicely. Many thanks."

Post: The Torrington Jewish Houses Of Worship

Some of you might recall that a couple of days ago I recounted an incident in which I was asked (while I was mowing the front yard) by a couple of passing motorists if there was a synagogue in Torrington. I told them that there had been, for a long time, but no more. This brief exchange got me wondering about the history of Jewish houses of worship in Torrington. Here's what I found out. . . Back in the 1890s, most of the few Torrington Jewish families were Orthodox and worshiped in each other's homes. That changed in 1910 when they purchased property on East Main and called it the Sons Of Jacob Congregation. In 1918 the congregation moved to an old Swedish church on Spear Street, where the downtown shopping plaza is today, and 4 years later they started the town's first Hebrew school. A man named Harry Radunsky was one of the earliest spiritual leaders and taught children, like a young Abe Temkin, to read and write Hebrew.

(Above, Hebrew school students in 1931 gather for a party. Top Row, L-R: Julie Harris and Harry Radom. Middle Row: Edythe Garbus, Isabel Jaffe, Helen Goluboff, Anna Baker, Minnie Baker, Ida Jaffee. Front Row: Gertrude Brenner, Seymour Robinson, Lillian Morganstein, Jack Goldman, Frances Sirkin [standing], Sylvia Lessow.)

In 1942 the congregation, now called Beth El (a merger/compromise of the more Orthodox Jews with those seeing themselves as modern

Reformers), bought the Brooke mansion and land on Litchfield Street. In 1950 a wing was added (pictured below), and in 1958 the

original mansion was razed in order to add office space and a library. During the succeeding years, and for several decades, the synagogue thrived. Attendance went up, children filled the school, and there was an active social scene with a men's club, a women's club, a veterans group, a boy scout troop, and dances and parties. Members ran a gift shop and maintained a library. They put together a cook book and held at least one major TAG sale. I vividly recall buying a couple of HUGE stand-up Christmas wreaths complete bases and lights, and having to tie them to the roof of the car. . . Beth El was the center of Jewish community life. People like long time member Jerry Libby (on the right as he appeared in 1957) had grown up in the synagogue, had been bar mitzvahed there, as had his 2 sons. . . By

the millennium, attendance and membership were in steep decline. In

2011 the Hebrew school closed when enrollment fell to nearly zero. In October 2016 the decision was reached to shut down the entire synagogue, and 8 months later in June 2017 the building and land sold to Iglesia Pentecostal Unida Latinoamericana for $225,000. The property would continue as a house of worship, but now for the Latino population, and not the Jewish community. Beth El was no more. . . I've always thought of Torrington as a receptive, open community where ALL were free to worship as they saw fit with no recriminations. My faith in that belief was only briefly shaken one time. In April 1990 vandals painted anti-Semitic graffiti on Beth El such as "Die Jew" and "Satan's children." To Torringtonians' credit, non-Jewish volunteers and businesses offered to help with the cleanup and add security measures. And Beth El members, in comments to the press, expressed their thanks and gratitude for this outpouring of moral and hands-on support. . . Beth El may be gone, but for the generations who worshipped and socialized there, it'll never be forgotten.

Responses included: "Great story. I didn't know the temple was closed. Sad to see all religions crumbling; the Catholics may have seen the worst. All these institutions served such great tributes to our community and now are almost gone." . . . "What a gorgeous former structure."

(Below, Beth El on a leafless day in November 2009. After the mansion was razed in 1958 and the addition built, this was the way the temple looked to generations of worshippers and townspeople for over half-a-century.)

"I remember attending services there. Did not realize it had closed." . . . "I remember attending a service at Beth El with Hugh Franklin." (Right, Hugh Franklin as he looked in 1966. Hugh was the son of Torrington teachers Seymour and Esther Franklin). . . "Interesting story. The Jewish presence was a major part of commerce in downtown Torrington and other communities throughout the US growing up in the 20th century. I'm thinking the malls, box stores, and

internal all contributed to their demise. Don't believe this has anything to do with the closing of Beth El, but as someone pointed out the Faith of our Fathers is no longer ours." . . . "I have many memories (with Jane Franklin, David Dan, Jeffrey Drucker and more) of causing great frustration to the rabbi during Hebrew School for our continuous antics!" . . . "I too was not aware that Beth El had closed and was sad to hear that. Many friends and neighbors were active members for years." . . . "I remember my friends Marion Peters, Hugh Franklin, and Emily Radler. I could not care less what their faith was, just that they were nice people." . . . "I spent more time at Beth El with my friends like Cheryl Richman than I did at my own church - St. Peter's. They had great Hanukkah parties with Wally and White as DJs (that's my recollection - could be wrong)." . . . "I did not know Beth El had closed. I used to walk by there every day on my way to school." . . . "I remember walking by and admiring it. It was a great synagogue!"

Two Frozen Moments In Time

(Above, 1951. A procession is held at Beth El to dedicate the new addition. The men are unidentified. . . Below, June 18, 2017. Less than 2 weeks before Beth El closed for good, co-synagogue-presidents Sally Bergad [on the left] and Joyce Peck pose one last time in the temple.)

A Few 1960's Teens from Beth El Mentioned In the Responses

Emily Radler

Jeff Drucker

Marion Peters

David Dan

Cheryl Richman

Jane Franklin

Post: Bill Goring, Torrington's Premier Book Dealer

Torrington's long time used book collector and premier dealer has passed (July 31, 2019). Bill Goring was not from Torrington, but he always seemed to me to be a native son, partly because he lived here for so many decades, but mainly because he helped put our city on the map with book collectors and intellectuals all over the country and world. . .

(Above, 72-year-old Bill Goring sitting at his desk at Nutmeg Books in December 2015. His desk was always cluttered with stacks of books, reference works, etc. and he was literally at the center.)

Bill Goring was one of the most interesting people I knew. He was a man of many talents, a multi-lingual off-beat character, a "left over hippie" in his own words who was just as comfortable talking about martial arts (he was an expert and had his own school in Torrington for several years) as he was discussing the merits of first-edition collecting. . . His business was Nutmeg Books, which he started when he first came to Torrington in 1977. His brother Albert was a lawyer who had settled here earlier, and Bill early on worked as a combination of office manager and paralegal for him. The book business was a part-time venture, and the first location was on lower Water Street right above where Quality Hat and Dee's Delicatessen used to be. It was a cramped space and only open Tuesday-Saturday, noon-five. After a few years, he outgrew the space, tired of paying rent, and also tired of lugging boxes of books up-and-down stairs. Bill and his wife Debbie, a medical secretary, bought a large house on New Litchfield Street, and they had an outbuilding the size of a substantial garage built in the back.

(Below, Nutmeg Books in the early evening twilight.)

This became Nutmeg Books, and soon was overflowing with books and to a lesser extent prints, periodicals, and general paper ephemera - the more esoteric the better. . . When I first started buying from Bill on Water Street back 40+ years ago, his clientele was primarily a local mix to include bibliophiles like myself and people just looking for a good inexpensive read. His reputation quickly expanded beyond Torrington to include all of Connecticut and eventually all of the country and the world. As the years passed and other new-and-used small bookstores were closing their doors, done in by the large chains, tv, and eventually the internet, Bill Goring kept Nutmeg Books going. He'd developed a large mailing list over the decades and knew serious collectors all over the world. He specialized in foreign language, politics, the occult, religion, philosophy, combat, weaponry, socialism, anarchy, and yes, even erotica if it was rare enough. The more unusual, the better. I once sold him a large box of vintage paperbacks from major motion pictures such as *The Hustler*, *Bus Stop*, *Splendor In The Grass*, et al. It wasn't a big ticket item, but Bill bought them for resale because of the great covers and overall rarity. I have no doubt he had them resold even before he wrote out the check to me; he was a terrific businessman in a hard-to-survive field. . . Bill was a stocky, powerful man, who over the years became more bent in stature and walked slower due in part to a lot of arthritis built up from all his years as a martial artist, jujitsu instructor. He had trouble raising his arms high enough to stock his shelves.

(Below, a few of the many stacks in Nutmeg Books
that Bill kept well organized and full.)

Though in pain, he was still a VERY strong man, a gentle giant with a distinctive Teddy bear quality, highlighted by a once dark beard and soft baritone voice. He emoted gentleness. He told me that it served him in good stead as a caregiver when occasionally the gents and ladies in his care at a local group home got violent, i.e. they might attack each other, but never him. Regarding Bill, THEY were protective. Sidebar: Bill worked for many years as a caregiver because, as he told me, it paid for medical insurance and gave him a pension. Bill was a dreamer/intellectual in so many ways, but he was also a pragmatist. . . Whereas in past decades I used to visit Nutmeg Books frequently to buy, schmooze, and perhaps have a cup-of-coffee with Bill, I hadn't visited much in the last 15 years. The reasons rested totally with my changed book buying habits, i.e. I buy now only what I'm going to read and even then have very specific wants in mind. I told this to Bill years ago, and he understood, though in retrospect I wish I'd dropped in more often, if only to socialize. I bought my last book from him 5 years ago. It was a rare, self-published autobiography called *My Story* (right) written by Susi Mark-wald. She was a long time New Hartford resident and a European by birth whose parents had perished at Auschwitz. It was a terrific read, and worth every penny of the $20 Bill charged me. As was typical of Bill, he apologized for charging me the double sawbuck, explaining that he had the book

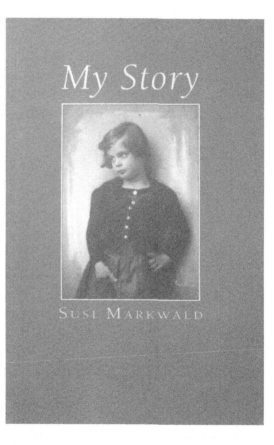

on consignment from the family and that it was a rock bottom price. I appreciated the apology and explanation, but both were unnecessary. Bill was always a straight-shooter, a fair-minded dealer with me and with everyone else. A good businessman, BUT, more importantly, an inherently good person. . . Bill Goring was once interviewed by a New York Times reporter, and he said, "I'll tell you something. Books breed when you're not there. Leave any two books together in a room, and suddenly there are more of them." Bill Goring leaves behind a LOT of books, both in his shop AND in his home library (10,000 in his personal collection alone). It's a treasure trove of paper, but the real treasure Bill Goring leaves behind is his large loving family, and his legions of admiring friends and fellow collectors. Rest easy Bill, and know that we book lovers will never forget you and the class that you brought to Torrington

Responses included: "Sounds like a very interesting man with whom you could easily spend an hour just talking about everything and nothing." . . .

"A wonderful bookstore, and a bright and genuinely kind and welcoming man."

(Left, a happy portrait of the broad-faced and Teddy bear-like Bill Goring.)

. . . "Though I hadn't seen him in several years, he used to come to the flea market occasionally and had a nice friendship with my mom." . . . "I knew Debby and Bill since 1977 when they first opened a shop at the bottom of Water Street upstairs. Spent many wonderful hours visiting with them both. I used to buy books cheap at the Salvation Army Thrift Store in Hartford and sell them to Bill (for a slight profit). I'm sure he did well with them since this was before I had a computer and lacked the ability to do research on my finds. When a friend of mine passed away not long ago, Bill came to his house and bought many books plus the bookshelves. I am so saddened with Bill's passing and will miss him greatly. It was good though to see Debby at Bill's wake and also to see his daughters and son whom I had last seen when they were children. Bill indeed had a great personality and was highly intelligent and knowledgeable in many areas. A great loss for Torrington." . . . "Bought and sold a few books from him over the years. Always an interesting conversation when we met up." . . . "Sorry for Torrington's loss. By the time that shop opened, we were in the twice a year quick weekend visit mode, and were not aware of the shop. Our loss." . . . "Very nice tribute. After reading I felt like I knew Bill myself." . . . "I had a close friend, who lived in NYC. Every time she came to visit me, she wanted to check out Bill's store." . . . "What a great story and a special tribute to a very exceptional and most interesting fellow. May he rest in peace and enjoy more books in the next life."

(Below, The Goring house at 354 New Litchfield. The book store is behind this, and the second line of the sign instructs: "PARKING IN REAR." A smaller sign would often hang below that which read: "OPEN."

Post: Torrington's Bookstores, 1885-1962

With Bill Goring's passing and the likely closing of Nutmeg Books, Torrington is without a bookstore for the first time since I can remember. That's a pretty sad commentary for a city of our size. . . Flashback: I did some cursory research back to 1885, and at that time there was one bookbinder and 4 sellers of books *and* stationery in downtown Torrington, then called Wolcottville. It's a safe assumption that books were sold locally before that. The bookbinder (M.W. Dowd) was at 107 North Main, and the 4 book sellers (F. Andrews, Baird & Renouff, C. Dean, and B. Marsh) were all centrally located on Main, the middle two practically side-by-side. The fact that they advertised selling both books AND stationery was not unusual, either back then *or* now. Seems that it's always been tough to stay in business for the shops that sold *only* books. . . Fast forward 15 years to 1900, and none of the 1885 book dealers were still in business. Instead, they'd been replaced by Clarence Dougal, Lucy Wheeler, Matthew Wheelan, and McNeil Pharmacy. Regarding McNeil Pharmacy at 98 Main (where Ida's Bridal Shop is today, across from The Pedlar), again it seems that selling books was a side venture and not the primary sales commodity for those who wished to keep the doors open and pay the rent. . . Jump 20 years, and in 1920 there was no one in Torrington who advertised selling just books. There were the McKitis Brothers *and* The Reynolds News and Stationery Co. listed under "Stationery and Newsdealer" in the "yellow" pages. AND, there was Frederick Clarke at 14 Water Street (see the photo on the opposite page) who also sold cigars, cigarettes, sheet music, maps of Torrington, school supplies, sporting goods, and daily and Sunday newspapers. Did he also sell *books*? It's possible.

Frederick F. Clarke
Stationer and Newsdealer
Cigars, Cigarettes.   Daily and Sunday Papers.   Sheet Music.

Telephone
14 Water Street   Torrington, Conn.

(Above, an ad from 1920.)

Sidebar: While there were no book-only sellers in Torrington in 1920, there were 8 pool halls and 21 saloons, which, I suppose, shows the priority of many Roaring Twenties males. . .

(Above, Frederick Clarke's store circa WWI, 1917-1918, probably around Halloween. Note the masks, the jack-o-lantern, *and* the sheet music and flags depicting a patriotic theme. Photo, Collection of the Torrington Historical Society.)

. . . Jump another 20 years to 1940, and there were no bookstores listed to the business directory. Under "Stationery" there were Lloyd Holcomb (450 Main), Torrington Stationery & Gift Shop (72 Main), and Jay's (formerly The Reynolds News and Stationery Co.). Regarding the latter, in September 1940 G. Morton Reynolds sold his business to Joseph Alexas. For the next 22 years until August 1962, Jay's would be the #1 book dealer in town. NOTE: It was advertised as both "Jay's" *and* "Jay's Stationery," and though there was no mention of books in either title, the store at 29 Water Street was *filled* with hardbound volumes in all genres and categories.

(Above, a cardboard ink blotter from Jay's, circa the late 1940s/early 1950s. Note the price of a new Webster's Dictionary was $6-12.50 depending on the type of binding chosen.)

It was a frequent stop for me back in the late 1950s and early 1960s. I walked to the YMCA almost everyday, and a stop at Jay's was part of the route when I had money to spend. I can still picture the interior. Bookcases lined the right side and back, while the sales counter was on the left. Did they sell things other than books? Damned if I know. I only had eyes for books back then, and Jay's had more than any place outside the Torrington Library. Towards the back right was the young adult section, and over the years I pretty much bought the complete series of The Hardy Boys, Tom Swift Jr., Clint Lane with its Army/West Point themed plots, et al. The clerk (owner?) would let me know when a new book in one of my favorite series was coming out, and I'd buy it as soon as it hit the shelves, then take it home and read it in a night or two. As I got older I branched out and bought the complete Sherlock Holmes, as well miscellaneous classics from The Modern Library series. One book that I still have is titled *Sport U. S. A.* It's a collection of the best sports articles that appeared in *The Saturday Evening Post* from 1901-1961. I inscribed on the inside cover: "July 1962, bought from Jay's book store." I must have purchased it the month before Jay's closed its doors forever.

(Above, 29 Water Street, Jay's old location. Today in 2019 it's a Tanning & Nails Salon. Ironic that a place that used to cater to the mind, today does a brisk business catering to the body.)

I had a small metal bookcase in my bedroom, and its shelves were filled with my "collection." Those books were my pride-and-joy, purchased with money I'd earned myself from my newspaper route, and mowing lawns, shoveling snow, raking leaves, etc. My mother gave the collection away a decade after Jay's closed, following my marriage and moving out. Years later I grew nostalgic, and over time acquired another complete Hardy Boys set (all with dust jackets), as well as the Clint Lane series. These 2 grace the bookshelves that surround the downstairs tv, and they're a daily reminder of youth and of a bygone Torrington that could support a bookstore.

(Above, part of a wall of books in our living room. The lower shelf that's visible here has been given over entirely to Clint Lane and The Hardy Boys.)

Responses included: "So it looks from the sign (first picture) that a person who sells stationery is a stationer?" . . . "Sadly, bookstores are becoming a thing of the past. The Hardy Boys series was great and another favorite was the Chip Hilton sports series." . . . "There's a nice new bookstore up here in Northern New England, if you're ever up for a drive." . . . "I love bookstores. If you want to do a fun road trip, go up to Saratoga some day and visit Lyrical Ballad - check out the website. There is also a newer one on Broadway; we were there last weekend." . . . "The closing of bookshops, new or used, stems mainly from online buying and the advent of Kindle. Shop owners could not compete considering the overhead expenses of renting, leasing, insurance, and the decrease in foot traffic. Many booksellers I know and knew gave in and took to the Internet." . . . "I bought books from Jacob's in the North End. They only had a turnaround rack of books, but I liked their selection. I too owned a white bookcase that I kept in my bedroom. I was proud of my books, and proud enough to want to keep them close." . . . "I was a Nancy Drew fan and still have a few very old Bobbsey Twins." . . . "I once had the entire Bobbsey Twins collection minus one book. I gave them all to a younger friend. Wish I had kept them." . . . "There was once a telling quote about judging a community by comparing the number of bookstores to the number of bars. Interesting analogy that may be rendered useless with the development of the web. You can instantly buy and read a book." . . . "Brings back memories."

Post: Torrington's Bookstores, 1963 - 2019

After Jay's closed its doors in August 1962, having failed, I guess, to find a buyer, I bought my new *and* used books here-and-there, to include driving into Hartford and New York City. And, of course, I bought most of my used books from Bill Goring and Nutmeg Books after he opened in 1977. Shortly after that, in 1979, Torrington was once again blessed to have a store specializing in *new* books when Michael "Mick" Tilbor opened Bookworks at 93 Main in 1979. Bookworks was just a few doors north of the Yankee Pedlar, and it could not have been more centrally located. Mick Tilbor himself was a wonderful person. Handsome and loquacious. Quick to smile, quick to dispense his knowledge, and quick to order *and* get any new title you wanted that wasn't in stock. Torrington was fortunate to have him. Between Mick and his right-hand girl Friday (Kathy Lovetere), service was A-1, customer relations top notch. . . Meanwhile, over at 274 East Main, The Little Book Shop continued in business. This business had started in the years following WWII. In 1947 it was called Cavanaugh's Little Book Store.

(Above, the corner site of The Little Book Shop at East Main and Maud Street in October 20, 2010. At this time it was The Candy Bouquet. Previously it had been an antiques store, and soon would be a print and embroidery shop called More Than Words.)

Mrs. S.R. Cavanaugh lived in that same block of buildings. By 1950 it was Stormont's Little Book Shop and remained so until 1958 when WWII Army veteran Joseph J. DiLullo bought the corner shop.

Joseph DiLullo apparently did not want his name as part of the business title, and henceforth the store was simply called, The Little Book Shop. DiLullo owned it till 1969 when he sold it to Conio Lopardo. Lopardo kept it going for another decade-and-a-half, but by 1985 The Little Book Shop was no more. I remember going there several times during high school to buy the Classics Illustrated a.k.a. the Classic comic book of whatever long-and-boring book we had to do a book report on. Sidebar: Because I loved to read and purchased a good many books even as a teen, did *not* mean I loved to read what the THS English teachers assigned. Rhetorical Questions: Did anyone really enjoy Sir Walter Scott's *Ivanhoe*? OR, George Eliot's *Silas Marner*? In any case, I remember that The Little Book Store had an impressive array of Classics Illustrated. Did they also have hardbound or paperback books? I don't remember. My lasting impression is that the store was more like a convenience store than a bookstore, despite its business title. Perhaps some of you remember more about this place. . . In 1984 Annie's entered the local book scene. Annie's was in the Torrington Parkade on the Winsted Road. It specialized in used paperbacks and sold them *very* cheap. I was in there only a couple of times, as I had little interest in paperback books, but I think a buyer got a discount off the already cheap price if a usable/saleable paperback was given to the store. Though the profit margin must have been slim, Annie's lasted until 2013, nearly 30 years, before it finally shuttered its windows and doors. . . There was also the Book Department in the old Mertz run by Helen Parnell for many years. It occupied a big chunk of the mezzanine, and it always struck me as a classy retail space, except for one thing. Because the Mertz hair salon was nearby on the mezzanine, the air was frequently filled with the odoriferous smells of permanents. Yuck! I could not find out when the Book Department opened or closed, but I seem to recall it being around in the 1960s and '70s. I'm confident I bought some books there, as I bought books at pretty much every bookstore I ever stepped into. But titles? Can't remember. . . In 1994, just to the right of Howards, Mostly Books and Cameras opened for business. It was a very small retail space and was absolutely crammed full, floor-to-ceiling with interesting vintage pieces to include antique games and toys. Ted Wanatowicz was the owner. He kept it going for 15 years, but in July 2009 decided to get out. In his words, the building had become "decrepit." He'd spent part of the previous winter without heat or running water (couldn't use the bathroom). He claimed the owners were in foreclosure and implied they no longer cared about him as a tenant.

In a sense he got out while the getting was good. . .

(Right, the small store front of Mostly Books & Cameras, just before it closed for good. It was just to the right of Howards, and was a narrow but long retail space. NOTE: The "Mostly" has faded and is barely visible on the sign.)

Though I don't think I've ever stepped into a "Christian" book store in my life, Torrington had one for 10 years. From 1994-2004, the Heart and Soul Christian Book Store occupied 3 different locations in Torrington: the Winsted Road, Migeon Avenue, and the Mertz building. The store offered Christian videos, books, music, and gifts, but in the last year, 2003-'04, after profits fell to the lowest point ever, owner Keith Douglas decided he'd had enough. He already had a full-time job as a resident counselor at a group home, which was what it took (100 hours total a week between the two jobs) to keep the book store going. It just wasn't worth it anymore. . . A professional bookbinder, a man originally from France and who had been trained at the Lycee Technique in Normandy, came to the area around 1987. Dennis Gouey opened his shop "and books too" at 36 Main Street in 1999. It was just up the corner from the intersection with East Main, and was definitely one of the most interesting retailers to ever grace downtown Torrington. Gouey in addition to doing quality bookbinding work sold antique books, bookends, bookcases, prints, first-editions, maps, et al. Needless to say, his wares were not cheap, and despite the unique nature of his services, he eventually bought a single family home on Main (approximately across from Dairy Queen) and worked his business out of there. Today in 2019 he has a booth at Wright's Barn and is usually there weekends, ever the businessman and antiquarian. . .

(Above, Dennis Gouey in a corner of his shop "and books too" in April 1999. His wares were handsomely presented, as was he himself.)

There was also an "adult" bookstore in Torrington back in the 1990s. It was called Torrington Book and was located at 466 Main. It billed itself as "An Adults Only Entertainment Center," and advertised: "Video Sales & Rentals-Novelties-Magazines-Papers-Pocket Books." I was never in the store myself so I can't speak from first hand knowledge as to what it looked like, the owner, etc. - not that there's anything wrong with adult entertainment. I don't know when it ceased business, but like most bookstores, it was probably done in primarily by the internet. . . Back to Bookworks and Mick Tilbor. Around 1997 Encore Books, a big East Coast retailer, moved into the Torrington Commons Shopping Center on High Street (where the old Brass Mill used to be). As is the case with most large box stores, Encore immediately undercut the suggested retail price on its books, which I remember was around $3 on a typical novel. It doesn't sound like a lot, but multiplied by hundreds of weekly sales,

(Above, a Bookworks ad from 1996.)

it quickly became the stake-through-the-heart of Bookworks. I
remember my wife shifting her allegiance from Bookworks to
Encore almost overnight to save a few bucks. And she bought, and
still buys a lot of books. When I sort-of gave her hell over it, and
practically ordered her to continue to patronize Bookworks, she
balked. I'm sure many locals did the same. It wasn't only the price.
There was simply the perception that because Encore Books
occupied a physically LARGE space, that it had to have more titles,
more choices, more diversity. Mike Tilbor assured me that this was
not the case. That, in fact, his store had just as many titles (40,000?)
as Encore, just not as many copies of each. Mick Tilbor also cited the
dwindling foot traffic on Main as a key factor in the decline of sales
at his store. Long-story-short: Encore put Bookworks out-of-business
around late 1997, and Amazon put Encore Books out-of-business not
long after that. And just like that, Torrington had neither Bookworks
nor Encore Books. Twenty-one years later we're *still* without a store
that specializes in new books. Want to buy a new book locally in
2019, better head out to BJs or one of the supermarkets. You can also
pick up a giant bottle of aspirin and a head of lettuce while you're
there. . . Gone, but *not* forgotten and certainly missed, are our
bookstores of old.

(Top Of Next Page, Bookworks circa 1997 as the going-out-of-
business process begins with 30% off all stock.)

Responses included: "Paul, what a great essay! Yes, the Mertz mezzanine was open in the 1960s. I think it was my introduction to a Torrington bookstore, being the source for most of THS's required reading. I moved to Torrington in 1963, and I shopped there frequently. Now whenever I dine at Slider's, I look up those stairs and remember." . . ."As goes the bookstores - so goes an entire industry. In the 1920s - hundred years ago up through the '50s - people waited on new books the way we wait on new movies, or something new from Apple. Twenty years ago Borders was packed every Sunday afternoon; today Borders is gone. Transition is almost complete, give it another 10-20 years, to Kindle, and other mobile screens. Who invested in 'Horse and Buggy' companies once Ford put the first Model T's on the road?" . . . "I'm not a Kindle user. For me the feel of a book in my hands or lap has a certain psychological aspect to it. In my current old age, I've become a Public Library guy. But I can usually depend on a store bought book as a Christmas present or a birthday present from my daughters. Yet I still love to wander through Barnes & Noble and look at the newest books. Back in my working days when my work schedule allowed an hour lunch, I would go B&N, grab a Starbucks (although I'm really not a Starbuck's fan), take a book off the shelf and read during my lunch break. I imagine I read one or two complete novels for the cost of a coffee." . . . "Excellent article, Paul, regarding a vanished business not only in Torrngton but in many towns and cities. Do you know what became of Mick Tilbor? Is he still in the area?" . . . "I know Mick went directly into real estate after Bookworks and worked out of Avon. He also had a weekend place at The Cape near Provincetown. He told me that his new career   HAD to be more lucrative than selling books in Torrington, implying anything was more profitable than that." . . .

(Right, Mick Tilbor in 2012.)

"Interesting. You know, I seldom ever think of the library when I'm looking for something to read. And yet there was a time when I checked out *lots* of books there, to include audio books-on-tape to listen to during my daily commute. Of course the idea of a bookstore furnishing you with an easy chair is that you'll comfortably AND briefly peruse a book, then *buy it*. Haha. Guess you can beat B&N, but maybe that's why the company's on tough financial times. BTW: A local eatery used to sell a friend of mine's books, until he discovered that people were regarding it as a lending library. People would grab one of his new editions, bring it back to their table, read a chapter or two, then put it back. Too many copies wound up with coffee and food stains, and had to be practically given away since they now had a 'used' appearance. Sorry folks, he used to say, but authors are not in the library business. Buy the book, or don't, but you don't get to eat a meal, or drink a cup of coffee over it." . . . "Very interesting. The first place I ever bought a book was at Mertz. I loved it there, in spite of the smell of the permanent wave chemicals from the beauty parlor, which was also on the mezzanine. The Mertz book department was there at least until I graduated from THS in 1967, as it's the only place I ever bought books in those years. I think I continued to buy books there summers, when I was home from college. I did buy books at Bookworks, and after they closed, at

Encore when I'd be visiting Torrington. In the past few years when I was in Torrington a lot, I bought quite a few books at the Litchfield Congregational Church, where they have a good-sized used book store which is open weekends. I believe that Dennis Gouey must be the man that I chatted with when we were sitting next to each other at the counter at Wright's a couple months ago, although I don't recall that we actually exchanged names. He was French and has a booth at Wright's, but we didn't talk about books at all. We talked about New York mostly. He was talking about missing it and moving back there soon; he was talking about still relatively affordable neighborhoods in the Bronx and the very top of Manhattan." . . . "Great article, loved Bookworks. If Mick didn't have the book that you were looking for, he got it for you very quickly. Bought a lot of books there and missed it when he closed." . . . "I met my wife at Mertz's bookstore. My aunt was the PBX (switchboard) operator, and I

(Above, a ground view of the Mertz mezzanine today. The Book Department was straight ahead. The Beauty Salon was to the right.)

needed a date for a college student body dance. As the VP of our class, I thought I should be there. My aunt escorted my future wife to the bookstore and introduced us. From there on it was history. She and I also frequented Bookworks, Encore Books, and a bookstore on Water Street that sold used books whose name I can't remember." . . . "Helen Parnell was another important Torrington book person. She worked in the Mertz bookshop on the mezzanine for many years, alongside Dottie Cleveland, wife of the store's owner. The Clevelands were wonderful people, really cared about their employees. After Mertz closed Mick Tilbor asked Mrs. Parnell to work for him. She loved working at Bookworks. I worked in the Mertz bookshop for a few of my high school years. Loved the scent of the old oiled wood floors in the place (but not the smells that frequently emanated from the hairdresser who was also located on the mezzanine!)" . . . "In *You've Got Mail* (1998 movie with Tom Hanks and Meg Ryan), the mega-bookstore crushes the corner bookstore (and almost a romance). If there ever is an updated remake, then Amazon would crush Hank's mega-store, but no one would go see THAT!"

(Above, Torrington's lone "mega-bookstore," Encore Books on a winter's day circa 2000. It was located in the Stop 'n Shop Plaza on High Street. To the right can be seen Opticare, Stride Rite, and the China Shop, the latter on the far right. Two of these businesses have gone under since this photo, and one has relocated. In the background Torrington Towers looms over the scene.)

. . . "So sad." . . . "How about just the ambience of a 'real' book shop!"

Post: Dinner On the Warner Stage

Ever have cocktails and hors d'oeuvres in the main lobby of the Warner, then move to the stage for piano music by Brian Pia, dinner, dessert, coffee, and sing-a-longs? Last night was the first ever "Dinner On The Main Stage," and it was a ball. You had to sign up (and pay) at the Warner Gala back in mid-May, but it was well worth every penny. I highly recommend it, and we'll definitely be there in 2020 if there's a 2nd Annual.

Responses included: "That looks like fun!. And you are with two lovely ladies!" . . . "Look at this beautiful crowd. You two young ladies look so beautiful, vibrant and glamorous!" . . . "How were the Italian cookies? . . . "Those cookies were magical - melted in everyone's mouths!" . . . "Looks like a great event." . . . "Now that seems a little different and fun!" . . . "I'll have to do that event when I'm back East." . . . "Awesome!"

(Above, L-R: Maurice and Judy Theeb. Karen and Paul Bentley. Picture was taken in the outer lobby just after the event ended. You can judge how much fun the evening was by the smiles on our faces.)

(Above, Brian Mattiello, chairman of the Warner Board of Directors, and Lynn Gelormino, the Warner's Executive Director, address the diners before the meal is served.)

(Above, long time Warner actor and musician Brian Pia playing the piano before dinner. Brian Pia has starred in many Warner productions, and starred in this one too, i.e. he played before and during dinner, then led a sing-a-long after dinner. As the saying goes, A good time was had by all.)

Post: Grocery Shopping In Torrington, or Am I Losing My Mind?

I'm in my comfortable morning routine the other day, which starts at the Good Company Coffee House or Nirvana, moves to the Senior Center, then takes me either to the bank, package store, grocery store, home, or some combo of the last four. Yesterday's a Stop & Shop day. As I journey the few miles from the Senior Center to the East Main location (below), I know I need 2 items. I know because I

wrote them down on my desk calendar just a couple of hours ago. BUT, I don't have the calendar, and I didn't make a written or an iPhone note. No problem. I'm confident that I'll remember them when I get there. . . The deli counter is just inside the door, and I know we need sliced ham,

though it's not one of the 2 items. I get a ½ pound of ham. Nearby is the bakery, and the sight and smell of it shake loose one of the two things - muffins! I get the muffins, all the time wracking my brain what the second item is. Finally I decide to do something I've never done before. I decide to walk the entire store in the hopes that visually seeing what I need will trip the memory. . . I walk past vegetables and fruit, seafood, meats, soda, canned goods, cat and dog food, cheeses, yogurt, eggs, cleaning supplies, milk, et al. But no memo-

ry's stirred. I make the turn at the halfway mark and come back past ice cream, frozen vegetables, books, flowers, greeting cards, toiletries, personal hygiene god-sends, gift cards, etc. etc. STILL no memory is shaken loose. . . I give up and use the self checkout. Walking to my car I'm obsessed with the forgotten item. I walk 6 parking spaces past my car before I realize that I've gone too far, physically and mentally. I'm really losing it. . . Back home I can't WAIT to look at my 2-item list and see what I missed. I sit down at the computer and pull out my daily planner. WTF! Say WHAT!? There's only ONE item on the list - muffins. Nothing else, nothing was forgotten. . . I don't know what's worse: not being able to remember something (which happens all the time). OR, thinking you can't remember something that was never there to be remembered in the first place. Sort of fixating on nothing, based on nothing, a.k.a. a hole within a hole. . . POSTSCRIPT: Six hours later I remember that I had INTENDED to write down "sliced yellow cheese, individually wrapped." But I never wrote it down, so now I'm wondering if this technically counts as a "forgotten" item, i.e. am I losing it, i.e. have I fallen into a hole, within a hole, within a hole?. . . Good News: I *did* remember the mocha chip muffins. . .

Responses included: "OMG, you're killing me! Mocha chip muffins! Every time I go to Connecticut I bring home a couple of dozen of mocha chip and pistachio muffins. I just bought new lockable large containers to bring more muffins safely home, LOL. They are the reason I bring the big duffle bag instead of just a carry on. It's cheaper than mailing them." . . . "I love the pistachio muffins. Or I did until I read that they're 600 calories a piece!"

(Above, half of the Stop & Shop muffin display. On this side are Blueberry, Chocolate Chip, Apple Spice, Cranberry Orange, Lemon Poppy, and Pistachio. The Mocha Chip and Double Chocolate - both personal favorites - are on the other side.)

. . . "But your recall of every aisle and what food items and non-food items they contained, and the order in which you saw everything is excellent. I wouldn't worry too much that you're losing it.". . . "There was something I was gonna respond with. . . tell ya' what. . . get back to ya on that." . . . "My wife and I do pretty well finding 'needed' items in the store, but finding the car AFTER the shopping is the challenge! In frustration and during the search, my wife will sometimes ask if we even brought the car. LOL!" . . . "Great way to start the day with a smile. Good to know I'm not alone." . . . "VERY typical for the age Paul. (Notice I didn't say 'our' age. LOL) Reading, I thought you were going to say the other item was 'don't buy ham this week!' But if it were me in your shoes, by the end of the search I'd have a full cart anyway! The fact that you can walk by all those items without buying is incredible!" . . . "You should have asked the robot. He knows everything. He was blocking the door of the Italian ice cooler yesterday, and when I went near it, he made a funny noise and moved away. They need more employees like him." . . . "I like 'personal hygiene god-sends.' Good phrase!" . . . "If it gets worse with age, then I'm screwed and very soon." . . . "Obviously you do not have dementia. An individual with dementia could NEVER have written such a tome. Once an English major always an English major." . . . "That's my everyday!" . . . "Been there done all of that! Luckily we live close enough that I can easily go back and pick up 'forgotten' items (if they're really needed in the first place). " . . . "I love this, LOL. Everyday of my life, Mr. B, I feel like I have the *Curb Your Enthusiasm* theme song playing in my head." . . . "You funny guy, you'll never ever lose it. What would we ever do without you. If you forget to stop at the Senior Center, then we'll know your memory is going." . . . "Hilarious! I can totally relate because I walk the entire store a lot trying to remember what was on the list on the kitchen table. I either end up remembering what it was right when it's my turn to check out (after having waited

in a long line already). Or, I don't remember until I get home. Hopefully, whatever it was I had forgotten wasn't part of a dish I was preparing!" . . . "Score that E-1 (sounds like everyone)" . . . "Hahahahaha! Happens all the time to me!" . . . "This is a very large club you have joined, Paul. You have my complete and utter sympathy. If I don't write it down, I'm lost. My remedy is to laugh it off and start over again."

Post: A Celebrity Visits The Thrift Shop

Possibly the best endorsement The Park Avenue Thrift Shop at the Sullivan Senior Center has ever had. . . So, as most of you know, my wife manages the Thrift Shop and is there much of the time. Often when she's NOT there, she's hunting other thrift shops, TAG sales, consignment shops, etc. for bargain items to buy for resale. She worked yesterday afternoon, so she wasn't there in the morning when the movie star popped in. That's him in the below photo partly behind the mannequin, with which he blends quite well. Star of *The Deer Hunter*, *Hair*, and so many, MANY other films, to include a small part in *Do The Right Thing*. Anyone recognize him? Bueller? Bueller? . . . OK, it's John Savage. JOHN SAVAGE! Now I'd like to say that he popped in for all the great merchandise the Thrift Shop has, which it does. BUT, his former sister-in-law was working as a volunteer that day, and they've stayed close. The t-shirted gal on the right is his daughter Jennifer Youngs. NOTE: "Youngs" is John Savage's *real* last name. She herself is an actress and musician and was in the tv series *Dr. Quinn, Medicine Woman*, among other productions. They were in Connecticut to attend a 40th anniversary screening of the movie *Hair* at the Avon Theatre in Stamford. It was a reunion of cast members and was followed by a Q&A. In any case, be sure to patronize the Park Avenue Thrift Shop. You never know who you might be rubbing elbows with. . .

Responses included: "A very fine actor." . . . "He's still very active." . . . "A great looking store." . . . "Before I even read your post, I thought he looked very familiar but couldn't figure out who he was until I read it. That is really very cool!" . . . "The Park Avenue Thrift Shop at Sullivan Senior Center is a wonderful place to shop. You just never know what you'll find!" . . . "Great actor. Was in the movie *The Mustard Field* with Ted Danson in 1978. A great movie, Harold Becker's first full-length." . . . "So accomplished!"

Postscript: John Savage and Jennifer Youngs join a long list of celebrities to visit Torrington. A few in the past have included Leon Trotsky, Admiral Richard Byrd, Johnny Unitas, Willie Mosconi, Richard Widmark, Barbara Bush, Christine Baranski, Paul Newman, Mick Jagger, Lauren Bacall, Ray Charles, Jerry Lewis, Shirley MacLaine, Rita Rudner, Crystal Gayle, Glen Campbell, Wayne Newton, Tony Bennett, Helen Keller, James Earl Jones, Tammy Wynette, and so many, MANY more. I documented many of them in my book *Those Glorious Torrington Days*. . . Parting Thought: One thing you can go-to-the-bank-on is that the rich/famous have come to our valley in the past. AND, they will continue to come in the future. Keep your eyes and ears open. . .

(Above, the male leads in *The Deer Hunter*, 1978. L-R: Christopher Walken, Robert DeNiro, Chuck Aspegren, John Savage, John Cazale.)

Post: Torrington Barbers and Barber Shops

Barbers. Stylists. Beauticians. Getting your hair professionally cut. I can remember like it was yesterday my first trip to the barber. I was about 5-years-old. We lived on Pearl Street. One summer's morning my parents decided it was time for me to get a "real" haircut. Previously it had always been crew cuts, short and bristly. I don't remember if it was intended to be any different this time, but at least I would be a big boy and not be subjected to the kitchen buzz cut. My father and I walked the few blocks to John Street, that little thoroughfare opposite the old fire station. Back then it was Ben's Barber Shop (picture below of the building that once housed "Ben's"). Later it would be Ugo's. I remember that the barber was a

kindly old gent. He smiled a lot. It was probably the owner Benjamin Fleischer. I was terrified. I did NOT want him coming anywhere near me with those scissors. When I got in the chair and he approached, I began to wail loudly! My eyes were riveted on those scissors. He backed off. He and my father attempted to calm me down. I think candy was offered, but nothing worked. Finally, my dad and I walked back home with scarcely a hair trimmed on my blond head. It took about another year before I ceased my irrational fear over barbers and scissors. . . In my youth there were MANY barbers to chose from if one wanted a cut. There had pretty much *always* been plenty of barbers. Going back to 1885, I found there were 8 barber shops in Torrington: Elty Brothers, H. Fowler, Gibbs & Ryan, J. Lisbon, D. Maynard, Poliquin Simeon, G. Rank, and M. Theroux. They were all

downtown on Main. One was on the bridge, another up the North
End. . . Over the decades, Torrington never had a shortage of hair
cutters, tonsorial artists. In a 1939 photograph (below, Photo,
Collection of the Torrington Historical Society) of the interior of
"Grandpa's Barber Shop," which I believe was actually the
"Torrington Barber Shop" at 181 North Elm, three barbers: Joseph
Adorno (on the left), Rosario DiMauro (middle), and Samuel Adorno
(right, son of Joseph) pose next to their chairs. They're dressed in
white shirts, white pants, and two wear dark ties. The space is well

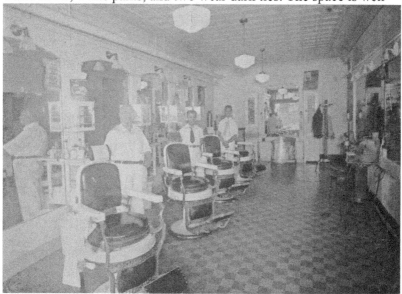

lit, clean, and well furnished with everything one associates with old
time barber shops: mirrors, various tonics, glass cabinets, a stamped-
tin ceiling, a checkerboard tiled floor, etc. It looks like a friendly
place; the type a male would patronize, not only to get a haircut but
also to pass time reading a magazine/newspaper and/or discussing
the latest news. Sports, weather, politics - the barbers I knew were
always willing and able to pick up the conversation, offer their
opinions, and somehow not offend. Good guys, friendly, congenial,
hail fellow types. . . In my teen years, in 1965 alone, there were
about 25 barber shops in Torrington which included in small part:
Andy's Barber Shop (365 South Main), Rocco Anzellotti (480 Main),
Joseph Bruneau (194 Washington Avenue), Chester's Barber Shop
(32 East Main), and Modern Barber Shop (24 High Street). Three of

my THS friends' fathers were barbers. Tom Piccolo's dad owned
Dom's Barber Shop (622 Main).

(Dom's Barber Shop was on the right side of these 2019 businesses,
i.e. alongside Zeller Tire Co. A tattoo parlor is in that space today.)

Joe Rinaldi's dad owned Al's Barber Shop (93 Franklin). And Buddy
Marciano's dad Salvatore worked at Park Barber Shop (135
Litchfield Street), which I think Joe Ricciardone owned. My own
barber was Louie Cantilena. He was a very pleasant man who owned
Anthony's Barber Shop, which was on Main near the bridge, then
moved around the corner to lower Water Street. It never occurred to
me to switch from Louie to one of my friends' fathers. There was a
good deal of loyalty when one had one's "own" barber, and Louie
had been "my" barber before I was ever friendly with Tom, Joe, or
Buddy. Beside, Louie Cantilena was the first person to ever use a
straight razor on me (back of the neck), and that involved a *lot* of
trust. One doesn't forsake such a barber lightly. I kidded my buddies
a few times that if I ever wanted to place a bet, I'd switch to their
dads. Such was the reputation some barbers had, i.e. taking a little
book on-the-side to make ends meet. . . When I got out of the Army
in 1970, I went back to Louie. Eventually he retired, and I had to find
another barber. I tried several including John Audia (also an
accomplished accordion player, portrait artist, and sign painter) and
Pat Scalfani a.k.a. "The Mayor Of the North End," who was also an
accomplished musician (trombonist with the Leo Liddle Big Band).
It was a tough time to be a barber. Ever since the Beatles had hit the

scene in 1964, young men were wearing their hair longer, getting fewer haircuts, and tending when they did to want someone who could "style" as opposed to the traditional crewcut *or* slightly tapered look. Eventually I settled on Pete Persechino. Pete had started at Fiore's Barber Shop, I believe, which had two locations, one on South Main and another on East Main. When I started with Pete, he had his own place on Main Street up by the State Theatre. I was in the Army Reserve at the time, so the type of haircut I needed fit right in with the "traditional" cut that Pete, and all the old-timers, were so adept at giving. Eventually he moved to 19 Wolcott Avenue and took up resident in one half of a small building just past LaMonica's. The other half was occupied by Nora DeDominicus Leikes who had a beauty salon. It was a perfect coupling, i.e. want your hair cut?

(Above, Pete Persechino and Nora DeDominicus Leikes on Wolcott Avenue in front of Pete's half of the building, circa late 1980s.)

Men through the left door, women take the right. I liked Pete a lot. He was a down-to-earth guy who smiled and laughed for most of the time you were in the chair. Only short coming was that Pete incessantly smoked, one cigarette after another. To this day I love cigar or pipe smoke, but definitely *not* cigarette smoke. However, barber shops back-in-the-day were repositories of tobacco smoke, mainly cigarettes, so if a fellow was going to get a haircut, he'd better get used to it. I said something to Pete a couple of times along the lines of, Gee, you sure smoke a *lot!* He'd smile and shrug it off. . . After Pete sadly died around 20 years ago, at first I just went to Nora in the other half of the building. Going to a beauty salon was no problem. A good friend of mine went to Anthony Boccio at Anthony's House of Elegance on Riverside Avenue for decades.

(Above, the old Anthony's on the corner of Riverside and Dale. Anthony "Tony" Boccio and his wife Patricia co-owned it. Like many old time barbers and hair stylists, Tony was Torrington born-and-raised and was a member of the Elks, Sons Of Italy, and Foresters, in addition to being an avid golfer and bass fisherman, i.e. he was well known around town.)

Nora gave wonderful stylized cuts, but soon wanted me to make appointments. She was booked solid and could simply not squeeze in drop-ins. Unfortunately, I seldom planned ahead for a haircut, i.e. when I wanted it cut, I wanted it cut. So, I began going to Don Marciano, owner of Modern Barber Shop at 368 Church Street, right where Pezze's TV used to be. Don Marciano (THS Class Of 1959) had been a barber practically since his THS graduation, working at one point in Waterbury. When I started going to him, he also had 2 gals holding down chairs. He told me that they were beauty school trained and that he had to further their education by teaching them how to give a "regular" men's haircut. Longer hair was now out, shorter hair in, i.e. the barber business was once again good. . . In the years I went to Modern, I seldom got Don. Men would willingly wait

(Above, Modern Barber Shop on Church Street just after the morning rush. The barber chairs were lined up on the right once you entered, while the chairs for waiting and the reading materials were on the left. Unusual Sidebar: That small building to the right of Modern was once a hot dog business in the late 1980s - see below.)

for him, and I always wanted a quick in-and-out, so I always took the first available chair. After around a decade, as my hair got thinner-and-thinner, I decided I was going to go with a buzz cut, and I didn't need a barber for that. Every couple of weeks I'd put the ½-inch attachment on the electric clippers I had at home, and give my skull a good once-twice-trice over. Easy and time efficient. When I saw Don at a Memorial Day parade during my buzz cutting years and I told him what I was doing, he smiled and called me a "cheap bastard." I laughed. There's some truth to that. . . I never tired of the buzz cuts, but my wife did. For the last few years she's trimmed my hair every month or two. I can tell it's time when she says it's time. Postscript: I started as a child getting my hair cut at home, and now as a senior citizen, I'm getting it cut at home again. However, a big part of me will always miss all those barbers and the barber shops I patronized over the decades. In part they were social clubs that for the small price of a clipping, you were thoroughly entertained.

Responses included: "I had a similar traumatic experience the first time my father took me. I was 16, and he was tired of looking at the long hair! LOL" . . . "My barber was on Water Street, south side, a few doors up from Main. Cannot remember the name." . . . "I used to go to the barber across the street from St. Peter Church. I would also go there after a movie to use their regular, non-pay phone to call home to have my mom pick me up. That way I could used the dime she gave me for the call for more candy. Didn't work on Sundays, though as they weren't open. Found out the hard way - LOL." . . . "I used to go to a small shop on Migeon Ave next to what is now the Board Of Education building, just down the street from Susla's drug store (now LaMonica's). The barber's name was Al Pesce. He was small in stature and didn't say much. I went there for many years for my buzz cut. Mom would tell me to stop in, get a haircut, and dad would stop in and pay Al on his way home from work. Things were sure different in the late '50s and early '60s." . . . "I first went to Frank Bruno's little shop on Wolcott Avenue. The shop was actually part of Susla's building. After Frank retired, I also went to Al's next to the old Migeon Avenue school, now the Board of Ed building. That was Al Pesce (he went on to run KFC on East Main). Al's had 'girlie' magazines, but they were hidden from us young men." . . . "I went to Al's (Al Pesce) on Migeon. Rode my bike there without my Dad one day. I wanted him to leave my 'side burns' on, and he told me my father always wanted them cut. I said to Al that my Dad wasn't there and I had the money, so do what *I* want. He left them long, and I went home happy. When Dad came home from work, I was ordered into the car, and we went back to Al's. End of story!" . . . "I also went to Al for a long time. I remember the magazines, and also the time he went outside in the middle of my haircut to have a heated argument with a guy on the sidewalk. He was a true character. Also went to John Audia and his partner Frank for many years.

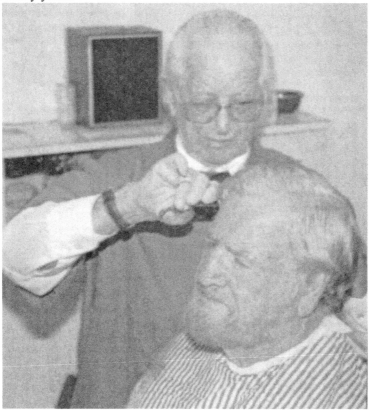

(Above, John Audia gives Ray Swift a haircut in June 1996 at John's shop at 520 Main. John Audia was a barber for 67 years and had a barber shop at several different locations in Torrington to include on Water Street next to P. Sam's, on Water next to Nicholas Pizza, on Pulaski Street, and on North Elm. Near the end of his career in 1996, he lamented the fact that the business only involved cutting/trimming/styling hair. Gone were the shaves, massages, scalp treatments, et al.)

Frank used me as a guinea pig to try his hand at the new thing called a razor cut. It didn't go well. I wore a hat for a few weeks." . . . "Pat

Sclafani was my next door neighbor when I was growing up. In fact, he used our fire barrel because he didn't really have a backyard. But I didn't get my haircuts from him. I used a barber shop right near Stop and Save. My Uncle Paul was always in there, so my mom sent me to him I guess. Of course, there was always a bunch of people in there, not getting haircuts. I think it was the first unofficial OTB in town, or at least in the North End." . . . "Pat Sclafani probably spent more time standing outside his barber shop waving to people than cutting hair." . . .

(Above, 57-year-old Pat Sclafani looks out his window in 1990 for some customers. He said that things always got slow after 1 p.m. His shop was on Main Street on Laurence Square.)

. . . "We went to the North End Barber shop for decades. When my dad became disabled, Pat Sclafani used to go to the house to cut his hair. One time at the barber shop across from St. Peter's, a woman announcer came on the air at WTIC. Another guy getting a haircut said that he didn't think he could ever get used to hearing a woman's voice on the radio. I suppose he did." . . . "My Uncle Ugo was a barber for years at Modern Barber Shop on High Street."

(Above, Roma Pizza on a winter's afternoon in 1996. This small brick building at the beginning of High Street used to house Modern Barber Shop. In 1965, the hair cutter's was on the right, a package store called West Side Package Store on the left. Mario Monti Sr. owned the liquor store, while Daniel Staino owned the barber shop. In 1955, a decade earlier, Michael Audia owned Modern. It's interesting to note that many of Torrington's barbers worked multiple locations over the decades, many going from hired help to ownership. . . NOTE: In the years I went to "Modern," it was around the corner on Church - p.119.)

. . . "When I was young, I used to go with my father to get his hair cut at Fiore's, across from the Bake Shop. I think he later moved his shop to the Plaza near where Woolworth's was. In later years, I remember driving my father to a barbershop at the top of East Main Street near where Bruni's Pharmacy was. I can't remember the barber's name (probably Anthony Capra with Full Fashions Barber Shop), but he was very nice and friendly." . . . "I used to go with my father when he got his haircut at Cilfone's on Main St. across from the old state employment building." . . . "Cilfone's is where I went too. I think his name was Mike Cilfone. When I was little I went with my father, every 2 weeks like clockwork. Eventually I went on my own. When I was 12 or 13 I decided I didn't want to go there any more, and my parents let me switch to Dom Piccolo on North Main by the Moose Head, because my uncle recommended him. I was still expected to go every 2 weeks, but the time between haircuts gradually increased, resulting in some real battles with my father." . . . "I grew up in the West End, and I remember my father telling me about a freak accident that happened to a barber shop on Church Street. A truck or car crashed through the front of the building. I don't remember anything more than that."

(Above, June 30, 1930. A construction truck owned by John DeMichiel & Sons rests partly inside the front plate glass window of Anthony DiPartogallo's Barber Shop at 368 Church Street having grazed the Fulton Market next door. This shop today is Modern owned by Don Marciano. The driver Thomas Baj had been traveling north on High Street when a car coming up Church turned sharply south onto High and into Baj's path. He turned the truck immediately to avoid a collision, which probably would have crushed all the occupants in the car. The truck was top heavy with 5-tons of rock and gravel. The back end drifted around, the driver briefly lost control, and the truck shot onto the Church Street sidewalk. Inside the barber shop, Anthony DiPartogallo was cutting a customer's hair. At the first sound of shattering glass and wood, he pushed the customer out of the chair and dove to safety. The building rocked on its foundation, but the truck fortunately came to a stop before penetrating the shop too deeply. A crowd immediately gathered, as seen above, and it took some time for inspecting TPD officers, Ernest Hurlbutt and Earl Bierce, to settle things down. Miraculously, driver Thomas Baj was the only one even slightly injured, suffering minor cuts and bruises. And though he was described as "considerably shaken up," he soon returned to work at the DeMichiel construction yard two blocks away at High and Central. It was reported, "A moment or two before the crash a little girl had emerged from the barber shop and at about the same time three other children had passed along the street. Had they dallied for a minute, all probably would have been killed." . . . Photo, Collection of the Torrington Historical Society.)

. . . "Alphonse DelMonte (Funzy) was with City Barber Shop across from St. Peter's Church and next to Petricone's Pharmacy. He and his family including daughter Diane and son Paul lived on Grove Street." . . . "There was a small barber shop on Brook Street below Sacred Heart Church. My dad always went there, and it was run by a guy named Santo. I want to say his last name was Italia or something like that. Does anyone recall this place?"

(Above, a photo from a news clipping in *The Torrington Register,* January 1982. Santo Italia enters his East Elm Barber Shop. This small building still stands and is directly across the street from the post office, though in 2019 it's abandoned. His daughter, Annmary Passantino, said that Santo spent more time in that barber shop than he did at home. That it was like "his little clubhouse." She remembered as a little girl "walking to the shop with my grandmother to bring him a hot meal of pasta and vegetables for his afternoon meal." Like all barbers, Santo Italia lamented the rise of The Beatles and long hair, and he was only able to stay in business until his death in early 1982 because of an older clientele. It was said that everyone came out with the same haircut, which resembled a military cut. Older customers were happy not to have to return too often for a "trim." Even Santo Italia's shaves were *very* close, and were claimed to resemble today's face peel more than a regular shave. His daughter said that stepping into her father's shop "could bring anyone back to the 1930s." . . . Below, barber Santo Italia with a customer in his small, but tidy shop. On the far left is a cash register with the words above it, "I WORK." On the far right is the "new" heater installed in the mid-1960s. Previously the heat source had been a potbellied stove.)

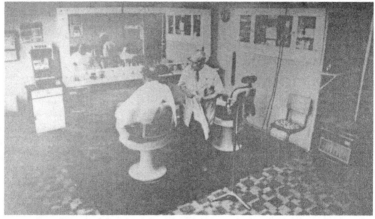

. . . "Great memories. I started at Fiore's on East Main, and Pete was my barber for years. After returning from the service, I went to Vic's in the North End across from Bill's Coffee Cupboard." .. . . "My grandfather and father were both barbers. My grandfather was well known for giving razor cuts and had a lot of female customers. He learned his trade in Sicily where being a barber was almost the same thing as being a doctor, as was noted by the barber pole and its history of being associated with surgery. On the other hand, my father hated being a barber. He worked for a few years cutting hair, then got a job at Hendey's which was the beginning of his industrial career. He eventually retired from the Torrington Company as a Chief Industrial Engineer." . . . "At Fiore's I recall Fiore and Pete Persechino, along with an older man Mr Sorrentino (early days), and then later Steve Van Deusen. Al Pesce's was mentioned and my friend the late Vic Melaragno (wife Mary DiPlacito class of '65) worked there before opening his own shop on North Main by the old

State Theater. Vic later opened a package store on North Elm near the Standard Plant. Wow, my mind still recalls these icons of Torrington!" . . . "I loved going to Cindy Weiman Cifaldi's Mom's in-home salon on Patterson St. for a haircut, then sitting in rollers under a massive hair dryer. The good ole days!" . . . "Such memories - and for me, it was waking up on Saturday mornings to the smell of that horrid permanent wave lotion. Oh it was nasty and would travel throughout our house." . . . "When I was small my dad took me to the shop in the north end next to Jacob's, across from the North School. The barbers were old Italians which my dad would converse with seeing he was from Italy. Later on it was Piccolo's. When I moved to the South End, I'd go to Andy's next to the Spaghetti House across from South school." . . . "Did anyone ever get their haircut from Jerry Manes who had a shop downstairs at the Yankee Pedlar? Well, my only memory of getting a haircut from Jerry was that it didn't turn out quite good at all. I think I had gone to him several times, maybe only a couple, but this one time (and it was probably the last), I came out looking worse than when I went in. In looking back all those years, I'm reminded of Fred C. Dobbs' haircut in the *Treasure of the Sierra Madre*." . . .

(Right, July 1991, 81-year-old Jerry Manes gives a haircut in his shop in the basement of The Yankee Pedlar. The space was one level downstairs from the bar. A pipe can be seen running just below the ceiling. This well equipped Pedlar barber shop had been in the basement since 1949. For the ten years before that, 1939-'49, the Pedlar barber shop had been in the small glassed addition on the front of the hotel. Gerry Manes had been a barber at the Pedlar all that time and had cut a number of celebrity heads including Paul Newman, Boris Karloff, Jackie Coogan, and Efrem Zimbalist Jr. In 1991 he remembered the good old days when he routinely gave scalp treatments and did mudpacking. He also remembered removing leeches from people, which were applied to suck out the blood from the sick.)

Miscellaneous Barber Photos - Vintage & New

(Above the former New York Barbershop circa 1989 at 538 Main. This small building was in the North End across from Salvatore Corpaci's tailor shop and The Photo Shop. At one time in the 1950s Joe Adorno was the barber here when he was semi-retired; later it was Joe Manes. Note that the sign in the window is directing customers to The Yankee Pedlar Barber Shop, where Joe Manes' brother Jerry worked. This wood-framed, clapboard sided building was built at some point in the 1930s. Back then it was located in the greater Litchfield area and served as a hamburger-hot dog stand near Bantam Lake. No one knows when it came to Torrington, but by 1990 Bruce Strawinski of Torrington was the owner, and he wanted it moved. He was offering it for sale for $1. Moving costs would be extra and were estimated at $500. The Torrington Historic Preservation Trust took interest in *not* seeing it razed, and eventually the town of Bantam bought it for anticipated records storage. Their own records building had been destroyed by a tornado in July 1989.)

(Above, Joseph Schifini's Barber Shop at 235 Water Street, circa 1919. Part of a WWI "Liberty" poster can be seen on the right. This barber shop was on the flats of "upper" Water not far from the intersection with Church. In later years it'd be Russo's Barber Shop owned by Carmelo Russo. The barbers in the above photo, in unknown order, are Joe Schifini, Carmelo Russo, Felix Tino, and Vincent Sortino. Joe Schifini in the succeeding years would own Schifini's Beauty Shoppe with his wife Margaret at 70 Main. Photo, Collection of the Torrington Historical Society.)

(Above, the Modern Barber Shop staff in 2018. L-R: Gerry, owner Don Marciano, Tammy. All three of these barbers/stylists cut my hair in the past, and all 3 were excellent. . . Below, Thiago's Barber Shop in the North End, a "unisex" hair styling business. Thiago's is adjacent to Two Guys Pizza and occupies the same basic space that barber Pat Sclafani did in bygone years, i.e. the old Laurence Square neighborhood is *still* graced by an adept hair center.)

(Above, Dale's Barber Shop on upper Water Street in the space once occupied by Grump's Soup and Sandwich Shoppe [owner Roger Arsego]. Dale's is owned by Dale Becker, and it's been in this location for 3 years. Dale Becker is a former THS football captain and a graduate of Torrington's now defunct Brio Academy Of Cosmetology. It's said Becker takes his time and looks upon each head of hair as a new conquering challenge, i.e. he's a far cry from the old style barber who only knew one style haircut. . . Below, another unisex barber shop/beauty salon - La China. It's in the North End in the same space that the North End Drug Store used to be, i.e. another prime example of the repurposing of retail space over time. La China specializes in all kinds of cuts and styling to include braiding.)

Post: Yankee Pedlar Memories

I loved the Yankee Pedlar and had many a meal there, and many MANY a drink there. No one knows if, or when, it'll ever open again. Very fond memories of late Friday nights sitting at the bar, schmoozing, and enjoying the old time ambience. What are your memories of the landmark inn?

(Above the Pedlar bar on a quiet mid-afternoon before the diners and cocktail crowd arrive. How many business deals were struck here? How many friendships made, and romances started and ended?. . .)

Responses included: "I worked there as a busboy and an occasional dishwasher. Then years later I sat at that very bar and had one or two cocktails with a lady." . . . "My older sister had her wedding rehearsal dinner there, and later my younger sister had her wedding reception there. Good times." . . . "I used to stay there every time I returned to Torrington, even in its last flea-bag incarnation. Bummer that it's closed." . . . "Such a cozy spot - quintessential New England. People travel far and spend $$$ to stay/eat in such places. It could be such a draw for Torrington. Such a shame." . . . "Judge Jim and Ann Hogan would take their niece, Pat Foley and me, the kid next door, to the Pedlar for dinner.. Made us feel very important." . . . "I didn't know that it was closed. It was my favorite 'Watering Hole' in town. In the years when I was able to come back and visit, it was the only place I would go. I loved to go there after a movie at the Warner." . . . "Every Christmas old friends and I would gather at the Pedlar for a mini-reunion. Good times!" . . . "I spent many a Saturday night there with Ann Marie, the singing Bartender, and Scott on piano."

(Above, Ann Marie Mulhearn Sayer on the left and Liz Riley Ebner, two wonderfully personable and wonderfully competent bartenders stand ready for business behind the Pedlar bar, circa 1995. Ann Marie did, in fact, sing professionally and to date has spent over 30 years performing and composing. Back in these years not only did the ladies bartend, but they also frequently had to act as waitresses too, coming around from behind the bar to take orders and serve.)

. . . "Every Christmas Eve we stopped there. Everything else closed at 6 p.m. in those days. It was always our last stop on December 24. It was always cool seeing some of the boys of the THS Class of 1970." . . . "Had many great times there. Nice place for a Saturday lunch in the winter. Was considered a high class restaurant back in the day when the Rubens brothers owned it. Beautiful place, but, from what I've learned, don't hold your breath till it EVER opens again. Sad." . . . "I worked next door to the Pedlar at Jon Marie for many years. I'd meet for breakfast there with my fellow employees back in the late eighties and early nineties." . . . "Have many happy memories of time spent there with family and friends, just having drinks or enjoying delicious meals. Our daughter also had her wedding rehearsal there.". . . "I remember when the 3 Rubens brothers: Albert, Arthur and Gerry, owned it, though you'd never see any of them in the bar or restaurant, at least I never did. I remember that Gerry had a photographer studio in the front of the building on Main. I think that's where he usually was, and it was probably his first love, not being an innkeeper. He took our yearbook photos back in the 1960s and was a very good portrait photographer. I remember that when I went for

my yearbook photo, he had a large black-and-white, framed photograph of the famous actor John Carradine in his studio. It was a helluva portrait, and he told me that Carradine said it was the best that had been ever taken of him. Too bad he couldn't have gotten the same results with me, but I don't blame him. There was a whole lot less to work with."

(Left, Gerry Rubens in his studio, October 1971.)

. . . "I used to go dancing there on weekends or at Memories on Water Street." . . . "I loved being there Thursday nights after the stores closed. If we were a few years younger, we could pool our talents, and money, and buy it." . . . "My parents met there in the 1940s. They were introduced by someone named Jiggs Donahue. I don't know anything about Jiggs - does anyone? I took a friend to the Pedlar after we saw *Gypsy* at the Warner, and she treated me. The next time I saw her I mentioned it and she said, 'Torrington! I just called my credit card to tell them I'd never been to Torrington and to please remove that charge from my card.' I laughed and laughed and laughed. She reached for the phone to call her credit card company to tell them it was a legitimate charge." . . . "Jiggs Donahue was a reporter/editor for the Waterbury Republican-American. His Torrington equivalent was Walt Gisselbrecht, and the men knew each other well. Together put out a publication during WWII called 'News From Home.' " . . . "I remember spending a lot of time at that bar. Nice place. When the Reubens owned it, there was a private club upstairs in the hotel called The Torrington Club, I think." . . . "They served a good burger back in the day!" . . . "Back in the seventies, a group from the Torrington Company would meet at 5 every Friday night for an 'attitude readjustment' organized by Charlie Sica. Then off to the Springtree. Fun times!" . . . "When I worked at Vogel-Wetmore, if there was an PA announcement that there would be a 'choir practice' at the Pedlar after school, it was the cue to meet for liquid libations at the grand old bar! Wonderful place and miss it so." . . . "Great spot. Defines what an old school bar should be." . . . "I read that the Pedlar has paranormal activity. The history is worth a read." . . . "When I came home to visit, my brother and I would have a drink on Friday nights at the bar. Had many great meals in the restaurant. I actually had my first wedding photos taken in the lobby. Can you imagine walking down those beautiful stairs!". . . "My friend and I stopped in Sundays after mass at St. Francis for tea-and-bagels. It was always fancy! I also stayed there after my father's funeral, and we had a fine-celebration of his life there. Very fond memories indeed." (Right, a room key circa late 1960s.)

135

Post: Lunch At The Yankee Pedlar on May 13, 1943

Ahhh, today's Thursday. In the old days that would have meant the downtown stores stayed open later, and downtown itself would be crowded with cars, pedestrians, and shoppers. . . Today we're going to hop into the Torrington time machine and warp back 76+ years to Thursday, May 13, 1943. On the p.138 is a menu from that date from The Yankee Pedlar (the date is on the luncheon specials). Let's pretend we've just been seated for lunch in the dining room off the bar (this section was added to the Conley Inn in 1940), and it's THIS section that's formally known as "The Yankee Pedlar." The hotel portion, with its own dining rooms/reception rooms, is The Conley Inn. . . So, let's be seated, and let's look over the food (p.138) AND the drink (opposite page) menus. I think to start I'll have a martini

with the im-ported ver-mouth. I know 50¢ is a bit high, but whatthehell, let's splurge. . .

(Left, a small etched drink glass from "Conley's Inn," undoubtedly pre-1940.)

And what would we be talking about in May 1943? Well, the page 1 news in *The Torrington Register*, when it's delivered later today, will be about WWII, and the news is mostly good. All Axis resistance in Tunisia has ended, US bombers are softening up Japanese resistance

136

THE LAW PROHIBITS OUR SERVING INTOXICATING LIQUORS TO MINORS. PLEASE AID US IN KEEPING THIS LAW.

MIXED DRINKS

Brandy Eggnog, with imported Brandy	.75
Brandy Sour, with imported Brandy	.65
Cuba Libre	.45
General's Breakfast, with imported Brandy	.75
Gin Buck	.35
Gin Fizz	.35
Gin Rickey	.35
Golden Fizz	.45
Horse's Neck	.35
Horse's Neck (with Gin)	.50
John Collins	.35
Lemonade	.25
Mint Julep	.60
New Orleans	.50
Oporto Flip	.50
Planter's Punch	.55
Peach Blow	.45
Silver Fizz	.45
Sloe Gin Fizz	.45
Sloe Gin Rickey	.45
Sherry Flip	.40
Scotch Sour	.55
Tom Collins	.95
Ward Eight	.45
Whiskey Sour	.40
Whiskey Eggnog	.50
Zombie	.75

COCKTAILS

Alexander, with imported Brandy	.65
Alexander, with South African	.55
Bacardi	.45
Bronx	.40
Champagne, domestic	.50
Clover Club	.45
Coffee Cocktail	.55
Daiquiri, plain	.45
Daiquiri, frozen	.50
Dubonnet	.40
Jack Rose	.40
Manhattan, with imported Vermouth	.50
Manhattan	.35
Martini, with imported Vermouth	.50
Martini	.35
Old Fashioned	.40
Orange Blossom	.40
Perfect, with imported Vermouth	.50
Perfect	.35
Pink Lady	.45
Rob Roy, with imported Vermouth	.50
Rob Roy	.45
Sazarac	.50
Side Car, with imported Liqueurs	.70
Side Car, with domestic Liqueurs	.50
Stinger, with imported Liqueurs	.70
Stinger, with domestic Liqueurs	.50
Suissesse	.50

SCOTCH WHISKIES

Bellows' Decanter	.60
Bellows' Choicest Liquor	.60
Bellows' Glenlevit	.60
Bellows' Partner's Choice	.55
Bellows' Club Special	.50
Bellows' Longmorn Glenlevit	.55
Black & White	.50
Cutty Sark	.50
Dewar's White Label	.50
Ballantine	.55
Haig & Haig, 5 Star	.50
Haig & Haig, Pinch Bottle	.55
Johnny Walker, Red Label	.50
Johnny Walker, Black Label	.55
King's Ransom	.60
Martin's 15 Years Old	.55
Martin's Original	.50
Ne Plus Ultra	.55
Old Rarity	.55
Peter Dawson	.45
Sanderson's Special Reserve	.45
Teacher's	.50
Vat 69	.45
White Horse	.45
House of Lords	.45

RYE WHISKIES

Carstairs, Blend	.35
Calvert Reserve, Blend	.35
Four Roses, Blend of Straight Whiskies	.40
Golden Wedding, Blend of Straight Whiskies	.35
Mount Vernon, 4 Years Old, Bottled in Bond	.40
Mount Vernon, 20 Years Old, Bottled in Bond	.70
Lord Calvert, Blend	.40
Old Crow, Blend of Straight Whiskies	.40
Old Overholt, Bottled in Bond	.40
P M DeLuxe, Blend	.35
Old Schenley, Bottled in Bond	.35
Schenley Red Label, Blend	.35
Schenley Black Label, Blend	.40
Seagrams 5 Crown, Blend	.35
Seagrams 7 Crown, Blend	.40
Signet, Bottled in Bond	.40
Wilson's, Blend	.35
Bellows' Partner's Choice, 5 Years Old Straight Whiskey	.45
Calvert Special, Blend	.35
Paul Jones, Blend of Straight Whiskies	.35
Imperial, Blend	.35
Hunters, Blend	.40

BOURBON WHISKIES

Bellows' Partner's Choice, 5 Years Old	.45
Kentucky Tavern, Bottled in Bond	.40
Virginia Gentleman	.35
Old Grandad, Bottled in Bond	.45
Hunters	.40
Old Taylor, Bottled in Bond	.45

SEE OUR WINE LIST FOR A COMPLETE SELECTION OF IMPORTED AND DOMESTIC CHAMPAGNES AND WINES.

(Above, pages 1&2 of the 1943 drink menu.)

in Burma, and British bombers dropped over 1500 tons of bombs on Duisburg, Germany, alone. Locally 68 tons of scrap metal were collected this past weekend according to Michael Scanlon, the chair-

(Below, pages 1 of the dining menu. Lunch specials on the left.)

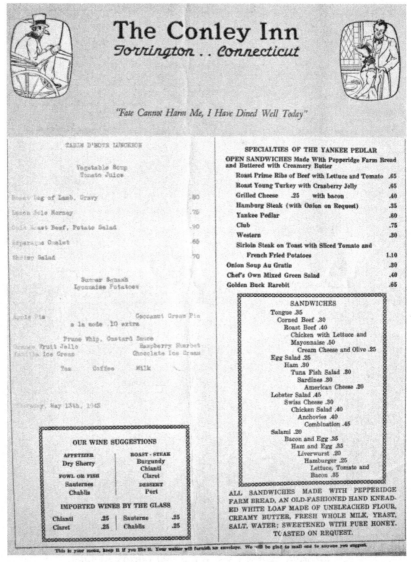

man of the Torrington salvage committee. Henry Poley just returned home from the South Pacific and brought back a few souvenirs: a Japanese shoe tree, tropical shells, and a Hawaiian grass skirt. These items are on display in the window of Bundles For America at 25 East Main. Aldo Rovero is attending army flight school to become a navigator, while Henry Kovacs, Joe Prevuznak, and Harold Herdt just graduated from other service schools. Sadly, William Bierce, a former captain with Torrington's own Company M, Connecticut National Guard, just died after a long illness. On happier news, Eleanor Jacqueline Jones recently married Master Sergeant Raymond Schaer. The sergeant is stationed at Hamilton Field in California. . . Are you going to order an appetizer? I think I'll have the cherrystone clams for 45¢ and a bowl of onion soup au gratin for 30¢ (p. 140). Yes, I'm hungry.

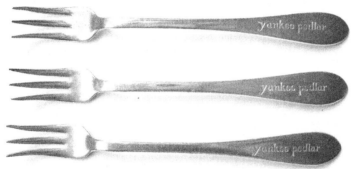

(Above, 3 vintage appetizer/shrimp cocktail forks from The Pedlar.)

. . . I see that Mertz is having a sale with ladies cotton gabardine coats going for $3.99, rayon stockings $1/pair, while cable knit sports socks are a good deal at 29¢/pair. Michaels is advertising that "true beauty can be wrought only in gold," and have a number of rings on sale including a ladies birthstone ring in solid gold (choice of stones) for $16, or for a big spender like you, you can buy a 14K birthstone ring with 2 side diamonds for $50. And remember, Michaels offers a "divided payment" plan. BTW: These clams are fresh and the soup delicious. Are you sure you won't have anything? That cigarette you're puffing must be killing your appetite . . . Torrington High just announced the Honor Roll, and 132 upper class students were listed. Of course junior Patricia McGowan is on high honors. SUCH a smart teen (she'll go on to be the highly respected federal Judge Patricia Wald, p.146). See anyone's else's name you know? . . . I see in sports that the Yankees are in first in the American League (13-6), while Boston's at the bottom (6-13). Dem bums from Brooklyn, the Dodgers, are in first in the National at 12-6. Wouldn't it be something if the Yanks and Dodgers met in the World Series! Of course, let's not count out the defending champs, the St. Louis Cardinals, just yet. Speaking of baseball, THS is doing great!

A La Carte

APPETIZERS

Cherrystone Clams .45
Fresh Maine Lobster Cocktail .50
Ripe Olives .15
Smoked Salmon Canape .50
Hors d'oeuvre moscovite 1.00
Fruit Cup Florida .15

Oysters in half Shell .45
Bismark Herring .25
Stuffed Olives .20   Mixed Pickles .10
Imported Anchovies on Lettuce .50
Tomato Juice .15

Crab Meat Cocktail .50
Green Olives .15
Celery and Olives .35
Sardines on Lettuce .25
Pineapple Juice .15
Cranberry Juice Cocktail .20

SOUPS

Consomme Diable en Tasse .20
Consomme Bellevue Cup .35
Onion Soup au gratin .30

Milk Oyster Stew .60

Clam Broth Cup .25
Cream of Tomato aux Croutons .25
Oyster Stew in Cream .70

EGGS

Scrambled Eggs on Toast .45
Poached Eggs on Toast .40
Spanish Omelet .55
Red Currant Jelly Omelet .60

Ham Omelet .55

Cheese Omelet .55

With Bacon or Sausages .65
Fresh Mushroom Omelet .60
Ham or Bacon and Eggs .65
Western Omelet .50

DIVERSES

Welsh Rarebit .60
Scotch Woodcock .75

Golden Buck .75
Canape Lorenzo .75
Creamed Turkey on Toast .90
Creamed Chicken and Fresh Mushroom Pattie .90

Yorkshire Buck .80
Minced Chicken a la King .90

Fresh Maine Lobster a la Newburg 1.15
Crab Meat Dewey 1.00
Spaghetti au Gratin .60

Fresh Shrimp Creole 1.00
Spaghetti Creole .65
Spaghetti Italienne .75

Crab Meat au Gratin 1.00
Fresh Shrimp Indienne 1.00
Spaghetti Caruso .80

FROM THE CHARCOAL BROILER

Whole live broiled Chicken Lobster, drawn butter 1.20
Whole live broiled large Lobster, drawn butter 1.55

Half a broiled Spring Chicken with French Fried Potatoes 1.10   Lamb Chops Club Style 1.35
Filet Mignon 1.40, en casserole 1.65   Steak a la Minute with Potatoes O'Brien 1.25
Sirloin Steak for one 1.50, for two 2.75   Spring Lamb Chops .90, single .45
English Chop (1) .60   Planked Steak for two 3.75, for three 5.50
Breast of Chicken Virginia 1.25   Garniture of fresh Mushrooms .25
Filet Mignon bouquetiere 1.75   Garniture of Onions .25

COLD MEATS

Sliced Breast of Chicken 1.00
Sugar Cured Ham .75

Roast Turkey 1.15

Potato Salad is served with all Cold Meats

Smoked Tongue .75
Roast Prime Ribs of Beef 1.00

SALADS

Crabmeat .90
Hard Boiled Eggs .50
Hearts of Lettuce .30
Asparagus Tips .60

Chicken 1.00   Lobster 1.25
Fruit Salad .65   Tuna Fish .75
Lettuce and Tomato .40

Shrimp 1.00
Combination .50
Chef's Salad .40
Mayonnaise or Fresh Dressing served with Salads

VEGETABLES

Green Peas .25
Stewed Tomato .25

Stewed Corn .15   Buttered Beets .15
Succotash .20   String Beans .20
Asparagus Tips, butter sauce .55

Lima Beans .20
Fresh Spinach .25

POTATO

French Fried .20
Hashed Browned .25

Lyonnaise .25   Hashed in Cream .30
Saute .20   O'Brien .30
Candied Sweet .30

au Gratin .30
Fried Sweet .30

DESSERTS

Pie per cut .15   a la mode .25
Fresh Baked Apple with Cream .20
Preserved Bartlett Pears .15

Preserved Kadota Figs .15
Coupe St. Jacques .25
Stewed Prunes .15

ICE CREAMS
and Sherbets .15

CHEESE

Camembert .25
Imported Swiss .25

Liederkranz .25

American Cheese .15
Cream .15

BEVERAGES

Coffee per cup .10
Milk .10

Pot .15
Buttermilk .15

Demi-tasse .10
Cocoa or Chocolate with whipped cream .25

Pot Tea. 15

(Above, page 2 of the dining menu from May 13, 1943.)

Captain Stan Alexander is leading the league with a .571 average (8 for 14), the Red-and-White are in first place (3-0), and THS also leads the league in team batting, averaging .365. Want to go to the game tonight at Fuessenich? The boys are playing Leavenworth of

Waterbury and the action starts at 6. We can sneak in some shopping and drinking after. . . I don't know if you bowl duckpins, I don't. BUT Valeria Mixcus is in the headlines after winning the "Champion Of Champions" tournament at Arcade Lanes. She rolled a 113-121-112, which is a new record. Catherine Considine was the defending champ, but she finished 4th. The men's tournament starts tonight, and "Checks" Balducci is the defending champ from 1942. Records are held by Al Marinelli (high single 165) and Chip Kemis (high triple 421). Guess none of them will be at the THS game. . . I'm not so hungry now, but I WILL have a shrimp salad (70¢). You love Pepperidge Farm Bread, which is all the Pedlar uses. What about a nice liverwurst sandwich? I know you love them. . . Any interest in going to the Warner this weekend? If we turn in 10 broken or scratched old records at McCoy's House Of Music on Water, (See the ad on the left from *The Torrington Register*, 5/13/43) we can get a free ticket to the Saturday matinee. Abbot & Costello are starring in *It Ain't Hay,* and it should be VERY funny. Sunday, a Lana Turner-Robert Young movie *Slightly Dangerous* begins. I DEFINITELY will see that one, but sadly the record deal at McCoy's won't apply. . . No dessert? No ice cream, jello, or sherbet? I think I'll have a piece of coconut cream pie. And I insist on picking up the bill. After all, you

haven't had a thing except 3 cigarettes and a Manhattan, and I can afford the 35¢. Care for another Manhattan? . . .

CANADIAN WHISKIES

Canadian Club	.45
Seagrams V O, 6 Years Old	.45

IRISH WHISKIES

John Jameson & Son	.45
Old Bushmills	.45

RUMS

Bacardi, White Label	.45
Bacardi, Gold Label	.45
Bacardi, Silver Label	.40
Bellows', Barbados	.55
Bellows', Cockade	.45
Bellows', Jamaica London Dock	.50
Caldwell's, Straight New England	.45
Lemon Hart, Jamaica	.45
Meyers, Jamaica	.45
Three Dagger	.50

GINS

Heublein's Milshire Dry	.35
Heublein's Sloe	.35
Booth's, Old Tom, imported	.45
Booth's, House of Lords, imported	.45

VODKA

Vodka, 100 proof	.45
Vodka, 80 proof	.45

COGNACS AND BRANDIES
IMPORTED

	Drink	Pony
Adet, 20 Years Old	.75	.60
Bisquit Dubouche, 3 Star	.65	.50
Bellows' Fine, 3 Star, 15 Years Old	.65	.50
Courvoisier V. S.	.75	.60
Denis Mounie, 3 Star	.65	.50
Hennessy 3 Star	.75	.60
Martell 3 Star	.75	.60
Monnet 3 Star, 15 Years Old	.65	.50
Remy Martin 3 Star, 12 Years Old	.65	.50
Robert & Fils V. O., 15 Years Old	.65	.50
Fundador, Pedro Domeca, 25 Years Old	.65	.50

SOUTH AFRICAN

Hugenot	.55	.40

DOMESTIC

Laird's Apple Jack	.40	.30

See Our Wine List For A Complete Selection of Imported and Domestic Champagnes and Wines.

(Above, page 3 of The Pedlar 1943 drink menu.

(Above, diners in The Yankee Pedlar in 1946. People are dressed up as was the standard for the times. Note the serving window was in operation back then. Sadly, there were no wall hangings, and the walls look stark in comparison to later years. The motto in 1943 was "Fate Cannot Harm Me, I Have Dined Well Today." It was printed on the menus and was prominently displayed in the dining room alongside an upper beam. It's still the motto today and still hangs over the dining room. Photo, Collection of the Torrington Historical Society.)

Responses included: "How many cherrystone clams do you get for 45¢? I like the liquor prices." . . . "It was probably a dozen clams. I know that 2 years after this, in 1945, at least 2 Torrington taverns were advertising a dozen clams for 30¢. I suppose then, as now, the profit was in the booze." . . . "Thirty-five cent martinis? Make room in the time machine for me." . . . "I'd go for the Irish whiskey (Jameson at 45¢), or perhaps a nice 20-year-old brandy/cognac like Adet at 75¢ or the 3-star Martell for the same 75¢." . . . "This was a fun read. Thanks Paul, and I'll have a Manhattan!" . . . "Enjoyed this. Oh, and by the way, I'll have a Zombie for 75¢ please." . . . "Just look at those prices! I remember Checks Balducci and Chip Kemis because my friend Joe and I bowled a lot of duckpins after THS. I even won a Class C tournament there. Really miss those good old days and ragging on Checks." . . . "The Yankee Pedlar was the place that I spent the majority of my downtown time in. It was a mainstay of down-town." . . . "My father used to tell me he'd dress up Friday nights after his shift at The Torrington Company, and go to The Pedlar to watch 'the fights,' the boxing matches. Back when most homes did not have a tv, commercial places that did packed the customers in on fight night."

(Above right, an original 22½ x 34" Conley Inn poster, circa late 1940s/early 1950s. There were two copies. One hung in the dining room *and* the other just off the main lobby going towards the north alley exit/entrance.)

(Above a very large, wall-sized Conley Inn-Yankee Pedlar wood sign, circa 1940s - 1950s. This sign once hung on the Maiden Lane side of The Pedlar. Today it graces the dining hall wall of a private Torrington residence, i.e. though no longer beckoning to the public, it still maintains a friendly and inviting watch over diners.)

Post: Patricia McGowan Wald, Torrington's Top Legal Eagle

There was a small news snippet in the *Waterbury Republican-American* this morning about the recent death of Torrington native Patricia McGowan Wald. Much longer items ran in *The Washington Post* and the *New York Times*. . . Patricia McGowan Wald made her mark early in life in the T.H.S. Class Of 1944. She was president of her Tri-Y club (Beta), performed 4 years in the Dramatic Club finishing as vice-president, spent 4 years in the Debating Club finishing again as vice-president. And she graduated #1 in the class, the Valedictorian. . .

(Left, Patricia McGowan's 1944 THS yearbook photo.)

According to *The NY Times* obituary; "Patricia Ann McGowan was born on September 16, 1928, in Torrington, Connecticut, the only child of Margaret O'Keefe and Joseph McGowan. In describing her childhood for oral history projects, she said she grew up in a crowded Irish-American household with an extended family of mostly women after her father left home when she was 2. While her mother and an aunt often worked as secretaries, the rest of the household revolved around episodic factory work at The Torrington Company. Her family, she said, took great pride in her academic success and made it clear that they did not expect her to end up on the factory floor. She went away to Connecticut College - it had offered her the greatest financial aid - but spent summers on the assembly line back in Torrington greasing ball bearings and fabricating sewing needles." Patricia McGowan went on to graduate from Yale Law School in 1951. She married, worked briefly for some of Washington's most prominent lawyers, then left the work force for 10 years to be home with her family and raise 5 children. When she did return to work, her successes only got larger and more impressive over the decades. She was the first woman to serve as Chief Judge of the Federal Appeals Court in Washington, D.C., widely regarded as the most influential court in the country. She also served on the International Court in The Hague regarding war crimes in the former Yugoslavia. . . She died of pancreatic cancer at the age of 90. RIP Patricia McGowan Wald.

Responses included: "I remember Pat. She lived next to my grandparents on George Street. It was a street filled with middle class, hard-working families. Such a smart girl. RIP Pat." . . . "George Street - very humble beginnings. I think Connie Donahue grew up on George. Sounds like an Irish neighborhood." . . . "I remember seeing her photo many times in my parents 1944 class book." . . . "What an accomplished woman!" . . . "She was a very impressive woman *and* a trail blazer." . . . "The write up in *The NY Times* is beautiful." . . ."For sure she was Supreme Court material. I wonder if she was ever considered." . . . "Wow!"

(Above, Patricia McGowan Wald is presented with the Presidential Medal of Freedom, the country's highest civilian honor, in 2013 by President Barack Obama.)

Post: The Day T.H.S. Burned To The Ground

Thanks this morning to one of our page members for the photo on the opposite page. Backstory: On May 24, 1913, the old wooden framed Torrington high School burned to the ground. Though the fire was of unknown origin, it was felt that it had probably been smoldering for several hours in some obscure corner before fully breaking out that Saturday evening. A number of people had reported seeing a "light" in the basement even before 9 p.m. Our local firemen arrived promptly when called at around 10:15 p.m., but given the amount of flammable material and the old-fashioned fire fighting equipment, the fire quickly grew beyond their control. Ironically when they arrived, all that could be seen was smoke pouring out of the building, i.e. no fire. Despite that fact, they quickly got six hoses/ streams of water pouring into the structure, but when morning dawned, all that was left were two chimneys and part of one wall. A crowd of thousands had watched the spectacle. The fire itself illuminated Prospect Street, and the crowd had to move to the east side of the street for safety. Along with the building, the contents were also totally destroyed to include desks, chairs, books, pictures, statuary (most of which were gifts from graduating classes), the lab equipment (microscopes, an induction coil, an 18-cell storage battery, mineralogical specimens, et al.), the 8" telescope and observatory, and so much more. Total content loss was approximately $36,000. Classes soon moved to the nearby Center Church while town officials prepared financing and plans for a new T.H.S. . . In the photo on p.149, a ceremony dedicating the 1914 cornerstone is being held. The contributing member says, "I do know that the photo is looking eastward toward Prospect and Main Streets in the distance. For instance, the St. Francis rectory on Main St. is visible. It is also a possibility that the child in the middle of the picture is my mother. My mother was born in 1902, and she was a member of the THS English faculty from the mid-1920s to the late 1930s. Her father died in 1916." He added that the gentleman in the foreground with the white hair *might* be his grandfather. . . The "new" THS opened on September 1, 1915. This would be the Church-Prospect Street school that would be in operation until April 1963, when an even "newer" THS was opened. Ironic Footnote: Even as students poured into the school on September 1, 1915, it was already too small. Positive Footnote: That 1915 stone structure is STILL functioning as a school today.

Responses included: None. There were no relevant comments.

Post: The Class Of 1913 and The T.H.S. Fire

How many students have said, or at least thought, Gee, I wish this school would burn to the ground! And let it catch fire before exams!. . . On the night of May 24, 1913, that happened, i.e. the old wooden THS on the corner of Church and Prospect burned to the ground, except for the brick chimneys, the foundation, and very small sections of the walls. Members of the THS Class Of 1913 were only 3+ weeks from graduation when it happened, and judging by the smiles on their faces in the photograph on the opposite page, they were not exactly grief stricken. In that photo, which I find highly amusing, eighteen members of the 1913 class pose amidst the charred ruins of their former school. Classes were almost immediately moved to nearby Center Church, so I doubt they avoided final exams. There were 28 class members total, and they were as follows: Mary Jane Twining (Valedictorian), Lena Maie Hills (Salutatorian), Katherine Ashe, Joseph Banasik, Mabel Bond, Ida Bowlby, Leslie Clark, Alice Cummings, Eugene Cummings, Edwin Dowd, Grace Emmons, Susan Gates, Margaret Hayes, Fannie Holcomb, Eleanor Kearney, Emile Kormann, Katherine Lawton, Catherine McCarty, Henrietta Meyer, Louis Moonshine, Burton

Morrison, Ethel Muller, Rose Norton, Augusta Osborn, Anna Palmer, Paige Seaton, Josephine Walsh, and George Weston. . . Unfortunately, I cannot put a name to any of the smiling faces in the group photo, and it's highly unlikely that anyone else can these 106 years later. . . On a very sad side note, class member Emile Kormann (left) died 5 years later in WWI. He was a corporal with Torrington's own Company M, 102nd Infantry when he was gassed and wounded in France. He died on October 4, 1918. He was said to be a "popular" member of the class and "well thought of by both his class mates and faculty." I like to think that he was one of the smiling students posing in those charred

(Above, 18 senior members of the T.H.S. Class Of 1913 pose amidst the charred ruins of their high school. Photo, Collection of the Torrington Historical Society.)

ruins 5 years before, i.e. the type of person who enjoyed life and smiled even in the midst of destruction. For sure, all the students posing in that 1913 photograph would know hard times ahead, i.e. WWI, The Great Depression, WWII, etc. But at least for one frozen moment in time, on a day in May 1913, they were a smiling troupe.

Responses included: "Looks like they had to step over a charred timber to pose for the photo. Nothing could stop them!"

Miscellaneous Photos Of The 1913 T.H.S. Fire

(Above, the immediate aftermath, a high school in ruins. The view is on a sunny day looking north up Prospect Street. . . Below, children and adults poke through the rubble. From these ashes would rise a bigger and better Torrington High School. . . Both Photos: Collection of the Torrington Historical Society.)

Post: Up In Flames - The TFD and Torrington Fires

Having recently discussed the 1913 burning of the old T.H.S., I'm going to hit a natural segue today and bring up the related topics of TFD history *and* memorable Torrington fires. My earliest experience with a Torrington fire happened in the early 1950s. We lived on Pearl Street, and one night a house caught fire around the block on Prospect, near where the Wall family lived. I remember walking over there with my father (I don't remember how he knew about it) and watching the firefighters work. I remember the darkness was mainly illuminated by the fire itself, and that a decent sized crowd had gathered to watch the firemen battle the blaze. Torrington fires always draw a crowd. In terms of major Torrington conflagrations, the Prospect Street fire wasn't much, I suppose, but it *did* leave an impression. In another 5 years or so I'd be sitting atop a fire truck at

the Water Street HQ, just a young boy enthralled with firemen and their apparatus, especially the pole they slid down. . . Many Torrington homes have burned over the decades, and probably over the centuries. In modern times, our neighbor's house across the street burned in May 2013 (Left, 2 TFD personnel prepare to climb the extended ladder as smoke pours from our neighbor's house), and though the house itself was not totaled, the family did move a trailer onto the property where they lived for many, many months while the inside was pretty much gutted and restored. Fires are always devastating to those directly impacted, even when there's no fatality or injury involved (and there wasn't with my neighbors). . . Formal firefighting in Torrington started in June 1887 when the Torrington Fire Department was first organized. It consisted of 2 volunteer companies: Crystal Hook and Ladder Co. and Excelsior Hose Company. The equipment consisted of a hook-and-ladder wagon (horse drawn), 2 hose reels, and about 2000 feet of hose. The 2 companies merged a year later in 1888, and the consolidated group was known as the Mutual Fire Company, Number 1. One of my ancestors, George Bentley (pictured right), was a Mutual volunteer. In 1916 the first purchase was made of automotive equipment, and the first paid fire force was instituted consisting of 5 full-timers. Volunteers were still used,

but in 1926 the Mutual Fire Company No.1 went out of existence when a city ordinance dispensed with the volunteer group and a regular professional fire company was formed. . . There has never been a shortage of fires in our borough. Prior to 1887, Torrington residents would quickly form a bucket brigade whenever a fire flamed up. It was a good communal effort, but highly inefficient.

Starting on December 16, 1887, the Mutual Company answered its first fire call at the old Farnham House. Less than one month later, on January 3, 1888, the company fought its first fire when a barn went up.

(Above, the Mutual Company firehouse on Water Street circa 1895. Below, the new firehouse not long after its dedication in 1901. Note that Water Street is a dirt thoroughfare.)

(Above, the Mutual fire fighters pose at some point circa 1901-1916 with their horse-drawn equipment with the "new" Water Street station in the near background. Right, a souvenir pinback from the August 9, 1901 dedication ceremony.)

From here on, Torrington's fire personnel have battled *many* blazes, quite a number of which were major. Though now long forgotten, the earliest major fires consisted of some of the following: Coe Brass

Manufacturing, March 1900 ($8000); Eagle Bicycle Manufacturing, December 1903 ($10,000); Lilley Block, February 1907 ($42,000);

(Below, the Lilley Block immediately following the 1907 fire. View is looking up Water Street from the intersection with Main. Claxton Drug Store is on the left. Both debris and water can be seen in the street and on the sidewalk. Ironically what appears to be an emergency call box is on the telephone pole in the foreground. Photo: Collection of the Torrington Historical Society.)

Perkins Garage on Maiden Lane, August 1915 ($26,000); Strand Theater/Opera House, February 1918 ($30,000); Agard Block, January 1932 ($50,000); Agard Block (again), February 1933 ($140,000); and so many more. (NOTE: Estimated loss is in dollar value at the time.) In fact, Mark McEachern of the Torrington Historical Society told me that sometimes it seems that there's scarcely a building in Torrington that hasn't suffered a fire at one-time-or-another. It was a fire on December 30, 1949, that destroyed my father's favorite Torrington theater, the Alhambra on South Main. Torrington firefighters were joined by companies from Winsted, Thomaston, Burrville, and Litchfield. The huge inferno was battled all through the night in temperatures that dropped to the sub-freezing teens. Ice formed on the firemen themselves and at least one nearby tree snapped because of ice buildup. Nearby buildings, including the adjacent First National, were hosed down in a successful effort to keep them from going up too. In addition to the loss of the theater itself, there were other businesses that shared the large commercial space: Hollywood Shoe Repair, Amy Maritano's Magazine Rack, G l e e s o n ' s Tavern, the VFW offices, a n d   t h e offices of the Brass Workers Union.

(R i g h t , p e r s o n n e l from the TFD fight the 1949 A l h a m b r a fire. F i r e - fighters can be seen on the roof pouring water into the blaze, while a lineman on the utility pole disconnects the electri- city. Glee- son's Tavern can be seen in t h e   l o w e r right corner of the building.)

Nothing could be salvaged from any of them, and losses were estimated at more than $150,000. . . In my own lifetime, there have been several major conflagrations that stand out: Bradlees (today T. J. Maxx) in April 1966; Gavlick Corporation (the old Brass Mill), July 1973; and Center Congregational Church, January 1979. . . The Bradlees fire started on a Friday afternoon in spring. It was first discovered by Elaine Iovane, a Bradlees employee. She was in the toy stock room in the basement when she noticed that it was getting unusually warm. When she went into a back corridor, she discovered flames and yelled out. The TFD was phoned immediately while several employees grabbed hand-held fire extinguishers. But they were driven away by the intense heat. Ultimately crews from Drakeville, Torringford, Cornwall, Goshen, and East Litchfield assisted. Trucks and hoses were all over the Downtown Shopping Center, while local police under Angelo Buffa and state police managed traffic and attempted to keep the crowds back. It was estimated that over 5000 spectators jammed into the South End to watch the fire, and it was feared that if the large glass paneled windows blew out, many people would be injured.

(Above, some South End spectators watch the Bradlees fire from the Fuessenich Park parking lot, i.e. it's the back and side of the retail store. On the left, barely visible through the smoke, is the Fuessenich fieldhouse, with a lone basketball backboard and hoop in the left foreground.)

Small private planes flew overhead to observe, and WTOR's Edmund Waller and Al Eyre broadcasted directly from the scene. Dunkin' Donuts provided coffee and donuts for the firefighters, and First National donated many gallons of orange juice and milk. First National was next door (just as it had been in the Alhambra fire, though now in a different location), and it was only a fire wall between the two buildings and the fire fighters success in keeping the grocery store hosed down that prevented the fire from spreading there. Embers were said to have drifted as far away as the Winsted Road. At one point the back wall blew out, and the first floor collapsed into the basement. During the evening O&G moved a crane into Fuessenich Park to pull out debris so that streams of water could be directed into the fires still raging in the lowest levels. The following firemen were treated for smoke inhalation: Deputy Chief Francis Yanok, Richard Thompson, Joseph Battistoni, John Smedick, Marshall George, James Ciriello, and Frank Lenihan. By the time the fire was out, Bradlees was totalled and First National lost its entire stock. Damages were over $1-million, though it was speculated that it'd be totally covered by insurance. Fortunately, no one was injured, but it was a fire that few would forget. . .

(Above, the curious gathered post-fire to stare at the collapsed Bradlees. The fat "B" of the sign can be seen bent back in the upper left, while the grandstand of Fuessenich Park is visible in the lower right.)

The Gavlick fire occurred on a summer's day in 1973, again on a Friday. NOTE: Although known as the "Gavlick fire," it actually started in the adjacent Connecticut Warehouse Corporation space. "But," as one veteran fireman said who fought the inferno jokingly pointed out, "Gavlick is just quicker to say." Like many who lived in the West End, I walked down to High Street, stood near the Hoffman

Street intersection, and personally watched the action down below, where today's Stop & Shop Plaza is.

(Below, the Gavlick fire as seen from the Water Street side. A-Squared Industries is the building on the left, and it still stands today. Though it's hard to imagine, if you stood on this same spot in modern times, you'd be on the ramp leading down to the Stop & Shop Plaza.The grocery store would be straight ahead. Below, firemen are coupling hoses to wet down A-Squared and other nearby buildings, while the huge warehouse wall immediately in front starts to collapse.)

I remember it as being a monster of a fire, so large that we onlookers questioned whether or not it could be contained, for it certainly could not be put out *or* controlled. If it hadn't been contained, all of Torrington could have gone up. BUT, it was contained, and firemen later observed that in many ways it was safer than battling a house fire. For this one, they poured as much water on it as they could, in addition to hosing down nearby buildings/businesses, i.e. they didn't actually have to stand on a roof or go inside as they usually did with private residences.

(Below, a water cannon shoots water high into the old Brass Mill. View is looking up Summer Street towards High Street. The former Hendey is on the left; Gavlick and the fire are on the right.)

In addition to fire hydrants, a nearby pond of 350,000 gallons was utilized, and thousands of small fish were sucked into the pumper and sprayed onto the fire. The fire got so hot that it burned off the paint on the side of one truck and melted the plastic rotating lights on top. It melted *and* twisted steel machinery and girders. Masonry walls collapsed. Though it was a calm July night with little wind, a thermal column of hot air (like a tornado) swept up dirt and debris and flung it far-and-wide. One spectator described it as looking like Niagara Falls, "except instead of water, it was all flames." Debris was found as far away as the Canton Golf Course. Ultimately 17 fire companies responded to the fire alarm, and the final loss in dollars was estimated at $10-million. The cause was never determined, and some always felt that arson was likely, though it was never proven. Positive Notes: The fire *was* contained and no other buildings were damaged, e.g. the nearby Torrington Towers, Hotchkiss Brothers, A-Squared Industries, etc. I myself salvaged enough bricks during the later cleanup of the site to construct a nice free-standing barbecue "pit" at our house on Spring Street. Unfortunately I couldn't take it with me when we moved in '78. . .

(Below, youthful volunteers on Summer Street help exhausted firemen continue to pour water into the complex as the fire winds down.)

The Center Congregational Church fire in the winter of 1979 was probably most memorable, not because it happened in the dead of winter or that it totaled a Torrington Church. St. Paul's Lutheran had suffered the same demise in August 1951 when it was located on South Main next to Coe Park. Center Congregational was most memorable because of its bizarre origin. Turns out the fire was set as a diversionary tactic to keep city personnel busy while the two young men who had set it robbed Hubert's Jewelry Store on Water Street. The fire itself (*again* on a Friday) was battled through the night in freezing weather. Unusual for a Torrington fire, only about 130 spectators stood nearby to watch. One was Dorothea Cramer, former head Torrington librarian who at 76-years-old *and* in the wee hours not long after midnight *and* in the dead of winter, had walked over from her home on Pearl Street to eyewitness history. She told a reporter, "I never expected anything terrible like that would happen. I can't believe I'm standing here watching it."

(Below, firemen battle the Center Church fire at night and in freezing temperatures. Snow can be seen on the ground. The firemen caught here in action include Lt. Rougeot, Lt. Herpich, and Private Nickerson.)

Flames shot from the windows and roof. The steeple fell flaming to the ground. The entire scene was illuminated by an eerie orange glow. City Hall was opened to give shelter to those needing a warm respite. Mayor Hodges Waldron, himself a deacon of the church, kept a vigil as close to the church as possible. He'd grown up in that church. Center's pastor, Rev. Raymond Shoop, kept watch from across the street and said he was "heartsick." The night wore on, but by 5 a.m. it was over. Everything destroyed but the ice-covered granite walls. Stained glass windows - melted. Interior wooden pews and   paneling - burned. Nothing left but the stone shell of the building. City trucks plowed the streets to clear away the ice and slush. By 5:30 a.m. the scene was under control, and firemen returned to their station. Postscript: Some regarded Center

Congregational as *the* most beautiful church in Torrington. They would not be let down for long. Like a phoenix, it would rise again from the ashes, perhaps architecturally even more beautiful than before. . . SO, many fires. SO, much damage. SO many Torrington businesses never the same again. In a 20 year period, between 1963 - 1983, some of the commercial properties/businesses that combusted included: Capitol Restaurant, Hewitt's Garage, Chapin's Package Store, The Place, The Moose Club, Iffland Lumber Yard, City Diner, Gabriella's Market, Vederame's Restaurant, Valley Park Restaurant,

Dialtone Lounge, Dunkin' Donuts, Moscarillo's, Palermo, Caldor, Jacob's, Acton Upholstering Company, Charter Oak, Santoro's Cleaners, Yankee Pedlar, THS (the little theater), Red Rooster, Leo's Cafe, the Torrington Country Club, and the Pig & Whistle Pub.

(Left, the original Pig & Whistle Pub wooden sign. Salvaged, but in rough shape.)

Many more have suffered partial or total fire loss since 1983. Epilogue: Over its history, Torrington has been changed by *both* fire *and* flood, though undoubtedly more by fire. Purification by heat and flame. City residents and property owners always pick up and carry on. Life goes on, and so does Torrington.

Responses included: "I was a student at Gilbert at the time of the Bradlees fire, and I remember seeing the smoke all the way in Winsted from the school!" . . . "Great post, Paul. My memories pretty much parallel yours, except I learned about the later fires from my Mom, having long since moved away. I remember going down to see the ice-covered Alhambra with Dad, and I witnessed the Lutheran church fire, at least until Mom finished her shopping at First National and we went home."

(Below, a crowd watches the August 29, 1951, St. Paul's Lutheran Church fire on South Main. At this time the church bordered Coe Park to the south. Behind the crowd, the back of the Fuessenich Park fieldhouse is slightly visible, as is a solitary Fuessenich light pole. Photo: Collection of the Torrington Historical Society.)

. . . "If I remember correctly, the Bradlees fire broke out while we were still in class at THS, and we could see the smoke from our classroom. The July 1973 fire occurred the night before my best friend's wedding. Since we had since moved out-of-state, I stayed at my grandmother's home on Turner Ave. From there, we had 'front row seats' to the fire. Of course, I ended up at the hospital due to smoke inhalation, but managed to recover nicely for the wedding on Saturday. Will never forget that one!" . . . "I was in 8th grade at Vogel School when the Bradlees fire broke out. We all started staring out the window and saw the smoke. School ended shortly after, and we all started walking towards downtown until we came upon it. I think everybody in Torrington at one-point-or-another caught a piece of Gavlick. I guess I was one of the 130 spectators that watched the Center Congregational steeple fall that night. I was coming down East Main Street after a night of playing poker. It was around 2ish. Anyway, I saw the glow and realized something was on fire. When I reached the bottom of East Main, I turned right and pulled over when

I saw it. I got out of my car, and it was freakin' cold! I told myself I'd have to wait until the steeple fell, and I did. Kind of morbid, I know."

(Left, Center Church ablaze. The fire has burned right through the roof, and the steeple is about to fall.)

. . . "I watched the Gavlick fire from our third floor apartment on Seymour Street. It was so scary, being so close. And especially trying to assure two little ones that all was going to be OK. Luckily we suffered no side affects, except for the lasting smell of smoke-filled air."

(Above, an unidentified High Street resident wets down the roof of his garage as a precaution during the Gavlick fire.)

. . . "I remember the Gavlick fire well because we were playing a softball game at Oliver Wolcott when ash started raining down on the field. Rob Koury and his brother Maron were there. They found out that the fire was at-or-near their store at the Water Street/Church Street intersection and figured that their mother was probably there. The game was called, and they drove down there immediately." . . .

(Below, firemen wet down the roof of Hotchkiss Brothers during the Gavlick fire. A-Squared Industries is in the upper left corner. The Water-Church intersection where the Koury store was, was a short ways up the street from this scene.)

"I was working at Howard's when Bradlees burned. We watched the fire from the roof of our building. I'll never forget the huge wave of fire that came out the front of Bradlees. The Torrington Country Club fire left us using a tent for a clubhouse for a few years, but we still had a great time. The Gavlick fire occurred the night before my friend's wedding. All of us guys in the wedding party left the rehearsal to watch the fire. The girls weren't happy." . . . "This post brought back many memories. The Center Congregational Church was the one I'm most familiar with. We investigated the fire and were there throughout the night and well into the following day when we made the arrest of the 2nd suspect over in Bristol, where we had tracked him to. The suspects that we arrested for starting the fire had taken an ice chopper from the church, broke off the metal head from the wooden handle and used that to break into the Jewelry store. After finding the metal head at the store with the wooden handle broken off, we were aware of the fact that when the fire at the church had first been observed, one of the doors on the south end of the front of the church had appeared to be propped open. I asked Chief Yanok if they had located, or observed, anything holding that door open when they had first come onto the scene. He himself then approached the door in question. Mind you, the fire was still going very strongly at this time. He returned a short while later with a long wooden handle that he located near that door that *did* in fact have whatever was affixed to one end, broken off. After a later forensic examination of both pieces, it was determined that the metal ice chopper had been broken off of *that* wooden handle. I have to say that while I always had great respect for the Torrington Fire Department and its personnel for the work that they did, I never respected them more than I did that very evening. They fought that fire on one of the coldest nights that I recall, and they were all covered with ice, icicles literally hanging off their helmets. Truly a night that I will never forget." . . . . "For some reason, I always assumed it was God burning that church because that's where my first unholy marriage took place, and he wanted to cleanse it." . . . . . . "Our family home in Torrington burned late in October, 1963. My mom, dad, and we six siblings were rescued off the roof. The firemen even rescued the dog. The house was destroyed, but it could have been so much worse. Believe it or not, we moved back into the house eight weeks later to celebrate Christmas. It always amazes me how Torrington people work together. From firefighters, neighbors, friends, builders, electricians, plumbers and family - stuff just gets done after a disaster like a fire!"

(Right, a vintage TFD Captain's badge, circa 1920-1930s.)

Miscellaneous Fire Photos

(Above, a birdseye of the Gavlick fire site after cleanup was begun. View is from the Torrington Towers. Summer Street is on the left, and the High Street Apartments can be seen at the top of Summer. The warehouse on the right is now gone, and this land today is the Stop & Shop Plaza.)

(Above, the blackened remains of the popular grocery store Hugo's shortly after the fire of October 1989 that destroyed it. A State Police fire marshal was called in to investigate. Hugo's was on the corner of Brook and East Pearl Streets. The building was eventually razed, and today the site sits vacant. . . Below, a boarded up P. Sam's Cafe after the December 10, 1999, early morning fire that ravaged it. P. Sam's was owned by Paul Samele and was a popular night spot. The building was eventually renovated, but sadly no businesses ever returned.)

(Above, late autumn 1999. Farewell messages are written on the sheets of plywood covering the burned out shell of Tombstone Cafe on lower Winsted Road. This building *was* rebuilt, and today is Dawn's Getaway Cafe. . . . Below, cleanup gets underway following the April 2014 fire at the O&G Warehouse on Albert Street, near Wilson Avenue and the Berkshire Cafe. The warehouse was being rented by Toce Brothers, Inc. to store approximately 5000 tires. The smoke from this fire was particularly black and acrid. Tiny particles and chunks of rubber, which went airborne with the smoke, littered the neighboring streets and properties. Piles of foam used to fight the fire lay like leftover snow. The site today is a plain of grass.)

(Above, May 1918. The 3 motorized firefighting vehicles of the TFD pose in front of the Water Street station. A 1918 American LaFrance pumper is on the far left.)

(Above, April 1992, 74 years later. The same 1918 pumper on the far left in the first picture is loaded onto a flatbed in South Windsor in preparation for its return back to Torrington. The intention was to make it a key display at the Northwest Connecticut Firefighting Museum after the old Water Street station was converted/renovated.)

(Above, September 2019, 101 years after the first picture. The same 1918 LaFrance pumper, now proudly owned by the Torrington Historical Society, sits on display.)

Post: The Camp Workcoeman Model

I was at Camp Workcoeman yesterday for the 95th Anniversary Reunion. In one of the scrapbooks was the below news clipping, which I thought was pretty interesting. The caption reads: "CAMP WORKCOEMAN SCALE MODEL, constructed by boys of Explorer Post 8 is on display in main lobby of Brooks Bank and Trust Co. Shown viewing model are, left to right, Lloyd Noyes, Tunxis Council scout executive; John Gawrych, president of Explorer Post 8, and Anthony Pasquariello, post advisor. Model will be placed in training center at Camp Workcoeman where it will be used for viewing and also as a guide for campers and visitors." . . . The news clip was undated, but I'm guessing it's circa 1959-'60. I

(Ocain Photo)
CAMP WORKCOEMAN SCALE MODEL, constructed by boys of Explorer Post 8 is on display in main lobby of Brooks Bank and Trust Co. Shown viewing model are, left to right, Lloyd Noyes, Tunxis Council scout executive; John Gawrych, president of Explorer Post 8, and Anthony Pasquariello, post adviser.
Model will be placed in training center at Camp Workcoeman where it will be used for viewing and also as a guide for campers and visitors.

don't remember that 3-dimensional model, though it sure looks like a terrific, and a time consuming project. John Gawrych was in the THS Class Of 1963, and after UConn and law school became a long time attorney in Torrington. He was also very active in politics. Sadly John passed in 2012. . . Do any of you remember this model of the camp? Any of you attend Workcoeman or the girl scout's Camp Maria Pratt? Have any memories you'd like to share?

Responses included: "John was a really great guy and friend for many years. I can't tell you how much it saddened me to learn he had passed away when he did and but I am happy to see that he is remembered." . . . "I had some good times at Workcoeman, having gone there two consecutive years and bunking in Tunxis, I believe it was called. The campsite consisted of tents on platforms. 'Poplar' was cabins. I distinctly recall buying an AMT 1932 Ford model kit at the Trading Post and entering it in races in the mess hall. One older camper had entered an empty Moxie bottle fastened with wheels and beat out everyone. I remember one event that was held at night. We gathered at the flag post in the parade field and attempted to reach one of the camp sites lit up with a camp fire without being caught by spotters situated throughout the woods. One of them, I think, was the son of the camp director Lloyd Noyes. He'd shout out if he caught someone, 'Go back, go back, go all the way back!' This was 1960. It was the first time I ever had apple butter."

(Right, a folded, Camp Workcoeman neckerchief from 1960. Most scouts wore the official BSA one, but these specialized Workcoeman ones could be purchased at The Trading Post, and lent a bit of individual style to the uniform.)

. . . "I earned my Second Class BSA pin and five credits toward First Class (never ultimately attained) during two weeks there in, I believe, the summer of 1958. I remember our campsite was way up hill past Poplar Grove (or some such name), and I don't recall the site's name. Tim Krom and John McGurk (both now passed) were in that Troop 39 campsite. During a camp-wide competition, Tim won the high jump competition (he was tall!), and I won the push-up competition with 39 (I weighed less than 100 lbs.!). This is when I first heard the scary 'Golden Arm' campfire story, which I later learned was a Mark Twain tale. Because our patrol failed to come up with a name on our own, we were assigned the name Worm Patrol. I passed my 'Swimmer' test but just missed 'Canoer.' At the Trading Post, I bought a balsa wood whittling kit and tried whittling an owl-shaped neckerchief fastener,

(Above, The Trading Post sits at the south end of the Parade Field in late August 2009, the camp season over. Though expanded and modernized from the 1950s-1960s, The Trading Post still retains the same basic look and still is a favorite part of camp life.)

failing miserably. I seem to recall camp was $20/week, and my parents allowed me to stay a second week but no more. I do not recall the scale model (in the picture), which may not have existed then." . . . "Outpost was the farthest out campsite back then. You're right about the $20/week back then. Today it's $450/week, but of course there are a lot more offerings.". . . "Oh, Geoff Noyes. I knew him in Troop 3 at Center Congregational. I haven't thought of him in many years." . . . "Does that model of the camp still exist?" . . . "I knew Tony. He owned Cesco Steel. Was an Admiral in the Navy Reserve." . . . "John Gawrych and I were classmates at St. Francis and THS. Mr. Pasquariello was a gentleman and Scout Advisor. His son Tony was in the THS class of 1963 also." . . . "I went to Camp Workcoeman in the early 1960s, and Father Bob Tucker was in charge of our group." . . . "Fr. Tucker awarded me the cooking merit badge. My wife says the only things I can cook are hot dogs and instant coffee." . . . "I was a camp counselor during the summer of 1965. I taught crafts, fishing, and marksmanship. Don't remember the that model in the picture, but I do remember the nightly nine/five games in the mess hall with the staff. Chris DesRochers was also a counselor that summer." . . . "I remember John Gawrych well. Our families were friends. He was a nice guy and tolerated me as I was 2 years younger. Great picture. Geoff Noyes was in my THS Class of 1965, and as I recall at scout gatherings, Lloyd may have been introduced as 'Loud Noyes.' " . . . "Tony Pasquariello was a Yale grad. My father-in-law, Major Cecil Best of the Army National Guard, and I worked for him at inventory times moving steel. He was a great person. Back to the scouts. I went to Camp Workcoeman for 2 summers. I was never a true scout, as I liked to go my own way. But I *did* learn to swim there." . . . "One overnight at the West Hill Aquatic Camp (directly across the water from Workcoeman), 6 or 7 of us decided to walk around the lake. We had to hack through some roughage north of Camp Workcoeman where Mary Frank and her family lived. We made it through and walked out onto a large flat open area. One guy yelled something derogatory about the scouts who were not far away in cabins. Not a good idea. The guy was a West Hartford trouble maker. About ½ mile south of Workcoeman a truck with about 20 older scouts, probably staff, barreled down on us. They surrounded us, and things got physical. They were SO pissed off. A few guys ran. They caught them. I thought: 'We are so fooked.' Seems that there was an arsonist who'd been driving the Camp Workcoeman people nuts. They eventually let us go, a little battered but okay. Next day the Workcoeman director called Joe Gargan, who was the owner and director at WHAC. Major international incident. Gargan decided to call our parents in for some horror-show punishment. But then a miracle, of sorts. I got a pass, and my KGB-trained parents weren't called. Reason: I'd been rushed to the hospital with appendicitis. Gargan figured I had enough problems." . . . "Camp Workcoeman was my first paying job. I worked in the kitchen under Barbara McKie, along with a few other scouts my age - 15, I think (age, not number of scouts). We didn't make a lot of money, but we had a great summer and plenty of good food. I also enjoyed being there during the two camps that were held before and after Scout Camp season - one was called Conservation Camp, where I learned to tie flies and caught a fish on one. The other was Music Camp, and the rehearsals were in the mess hall, so I just hung around and listened. Some of us went to the end-of-camp concert held in Winsted." . . . "Camp Workcoeman was also *my* first paying job, and I had to get a social security card to work there. I did a lot of growing up at that camp."

Post: Seymour Franklin: Teacher, Coach, Good Guy

March 5, 1969, exactly 50 years ago, THS teacher Seymour "Sy" Franklin died unexpectedly of a heart attack. He was only 51. Mr. Franklin was a popular teacher and coach. His son, Hugh, and his daughter, Jane, inherited his personable ways. I only knew him as the father of my friend Hugh, but he always struck me as a quiet, pipe-smoking man with a wry sense of humor, a person of quality. That George Avitabile was his friend says a lot. RIP Sy Franklin.

Responses included: "He was a nice man who fathered wonderful children." . . . "I still remember algebra concepts he taught us. Even though I was never a math person, I always enjoyed his classes. Don't ask me about my grades, though." . . . "Mr. Franklin was a wonderful teacher. Kind and patient. He actually got me through Algebra with a passing grade." . . . "I remember that whole week too well. I came home from school, as did several other friends of his daughter, to be with her. It was a family who made great contributions to T-town through their talents, kindness and love." . . . "Great golf coach." . . . "I remember Mr. Franklin well. He gave me a golf magazine which I still have." . . .

(Left, the 1966 THS golf team. Front Row, L-R: Jim Mordarski, Mike Dran-ginis, Jim Fass. Back Row: Coach Sy Franklin, Dave Brennan, Bill White.)

"Mr. Franklin was one of my favorite teachers. I was terrible at math but he got me through Algebra II. He was such a kind, gentle man." . . . "He was truly a gentle giant. I loved Mr. Franklin when I was a child. He was known as 'Sy,' and everyone adored him." . . . "He was a wonderful man. I loved him!" . . . "I grew up in the same neighborhood as Hugh and Jane so we played together as kids. Mr. Franklin was always funny and kind."

S. H. Franklin Dies Suddenly

Seymour H. Franklin, 51, a member of the Torrington High School faculty for 20 years, died suddenly yesterday in Atlanta, Ga., of a heart attack shortly after being admitted to Fulton County Hospital. His home was at 55 Lexington Ave.

He had taught in the mathe-

SEYMOUR H. FRANKLIN

matics department and was on a sabbatical leave, working toward a degree in guidance at the University of Atlanta. He also coached golf at the high school in recent years and at one time conducted the classroom phase of the driver training course. In his earlier years at the high school he coached tennis.

The son of Hyman and Leona Franklin, he was born in Freeport, L.I., Aug. 4, 1917. He was graduated from High Point College, High Point, L.I., and received his master's degree in physical education at New York University. Prior to coming to Torrington he taught in the ROTC program at High Point College for three years.

Mr. Franklin formerly was a member of the Commission for the Elderly and also served on the board of tax review. He was a member of Beth El Synagogue, The Torrington and Connecticut Education Associations, Probus Club and the Torrington Country Club.

Surviving are his wife, Mrs. Esther C. Miran Franklin; a son, Hugh J. Franklin; a daughter, Jane B. Franklin, both students at the University of Connecticut; two brothers, Jerome of Hollywood, Fla., and Gene of Lake Charles, La.; a sister, Mrs. Evelyn Schwitz of Hempstead, L.I.; and several nieces and nephews.

Services will be held tomorrow afternoon at 1 o'clock at the LaPorta Funeral Home, with Rabbi Joseph Heckleman of Beth El Synagogue, Waterbury, officiating. Burial will be in Sons of Jacob Cemetery.

There are no calling hours.

Memorial contributions may be made to the Heart Fund, PO Box 148.

Memorial services will be held Saturday and Sunday at the Franklin home.

Post: John Denza: Teacher, Administrator, Good Guy

News in March 1960. One of the nicest people to ever walk the halls of THS, John Denza, is appointed assistant principal (article on opposite page). Denza was a former Raider himself and his promotion came 20 years after his own THS graduation (Class Of 1940). John Denza was an upbeat, soft-spoken person, and I'm sure the news was well received at the time by students and faculty alike. . .

(Above, the 1966 yearbook, The Torringtonian, is checked over. Seated is THS Principal Richard Williamson. Standing, L-R: Arthur and Gerald Rubens, the yearbook photographers. Yearbook advisor Myron Root, and Assistant Principal John Denza. Sidebar: The 1966 yearbook was a state finalist in the first ever national yearbook competition.)

Responses included: "He made our schools a better place!" . . . "He ran the school. Did anyone ever see Mr. Williamson?" . . . "Such a gentleman!" . . . "Choosing John was a good decision." . . . "Mr. Denza was such a caring and kind gentleman." . . . "I loved him!" . . . "A true gentleman and leader." . . . "Top Shelf all the way. He practiced Zen without even realizing it. Now that's special." . . .

"Wow! He was an usher back when they had ushers at St. Peter's, and they also collected the envelopes and donations - bygone days!" . . . "Mr. Denza was great. He explained life from a teacher's point of view to me. He told me that my teacher was brand new and having her own adjustments to the responsibility of teaching. He made you look at things from different sides, and he was gentle about it." . . . "Our 1958 classbook was devoted to him. Proud to call him Cousin." . . . "I believe John died around 1989-'90. He suffered a traumatic brain injury from falling off a ladder from cleaning his rain gutters. I had the pleasure of knowing him outside school as I was friends with his sons Jim and Tom. It was not like visiting the principal's house; he was a great guy. His wife was great too." . . . "John Denza was a terrific man."

John A. Denza Named Assistant THS Principal

John A. Denza, member of the Torrington High School faculty since 1949, was appointed assistant principal of the high school by the Board of Education at a meeting last night. Denza will succeed C. Walter Johnson, who will retire from the public system in June.

Assistant Principal Denza holds a BS degree from Teachers' College of Connecticut, a master of

JOHN A. DENZA

arts degree from Columbia University and a certificate of advanced graduate study, University of Hartford, Hillyer College, with a major in secondary school administration.

He is presently engaged in his 10th year of teaching at Torrington High, and for the past three years has been assisting in the office of THS Principal Richard D. Williamson on a part-time basis. In addition, Mr. Denza has had six years' experience as a teacher in the adult education program.

Other Activities

His other school and community activities include: two years as freshman adviser on the school newspaper; 10 years as athletic game ticket manager; three years as treasurer of the Torrington Teachers' Federation Credit Union; recording secretary and treasurer, Torrington Education Association; fifth year as school cafeteria coordinator; fifth year as secretary of the Civitan Club of Torrington.

The new assistant principal is a communicant of St. Peter's Church where he has served as an usher for 10 years.

He is married to the former Eleanor Newberg of Rocky Hill and the couple has three children, James, Thomas and Janet. The family resides at 136 Northridge Ave.

(Above, the much loved and respected John Denza poses for his yearbook photo in 1961.)

Post: Southeast School, The Walls Come A-Tumbling Down

There was a short news snippet in the Waterbury *Republican - American* yesterday concerning the razing this week of Southeast School on Oak Avenue. The school was first proposed in 1938, but voters turned it down by a mere 73 votes. A Southeast Association was formed, and the group petitioned for a re-vote claiming that 15% of the "machine vote" had been lost due to faulty voter instruction. In a second vote in late 1938 the $115,000 Southeast School was approved. In 1939 the cornerstone was laid, and in the early 1940s classes began. At one point decades ago it became the Alternative High School and functioned in that capacity for many years. In 2005 the alternative program moved to THS, and the Oak Avenue school was leased for day care and after-school programs. However, in 2011 even those programs ceased, and the building lay vacant for the last 8 years. Currently demolition is underway, and when it's finished the land will be taken over by the Street Department.

(Above, the old Southeast School just prior to the start of demolition.)

Responses included: "I lived on Oak Avenue, and I am crying while trying to type my feelings. Seeing these pictures is heartbreaking. So many wonderful memories of my youth are gone!" . . . "I spent 3 wonderful years there as a teacher, having taken over when Mrs. Richardson retired in 1967. There were only 6 classrooms. Miss Alicky (Waltos now), Miss Vogellus (Shea), Miss Sugerak (Donahoe), Miss Sikora (Tobin), Miss Herpich (Perlotto), and Principal Marie Carrubba were the entire staff. Loved every minute of it! And I still see many of my students, and they remember all of us! So sad!" . . . "That is where I went to first and second grade before moving to East School. Sad to see how badly the building deteriorated." . . . "I went there for 6 years along with the rest of the Harwinton Avenue and Laurel Hill neighborhood." . . . "I spent my first five years of teaching in that building. Ate lunch across the street at Carbone's and visited Mr. Lovallo's garden next door where he cautioned the kids not to overwater the tomatoes and talked about the benefits of mixing manure in the watering can! Life sure was less frantic in the old neighborhood schools." . . . "I don't think it ever had a large student enrollment, but even today its former students think fondly of it. When I played basketball for Southwest School in the Elementary School League, we used to play games at Southeast, which had a far superior gym." . . . "We played our Forbes and Migeon games there also." . . . "I played many basketball games in that gym. Southeast and Torringford gyms hosted the grammar school basketball league back in the 1950s." . . . "In later years, the 1980s I think, a bunch of us rented the gym and played basketball there. It was a greatly underutilized facility."

(Above, the razing of the gym begins. Note the plastic covering the windows and the half-moon b-ball backboard still hanging at the far end.)

. . . "I'm wondering why it has to be torn down instead of being used for something else such as offices, apartments, a clinic, a shelter, etc." . . . "A $3 million price tag was cited to bring it up to modern code, which was prohibitive for reusing." . . . "I was just thinking, and realized that the majority of us went to elementary schools that no longer exist, although most of us can still see the buildings (converted to other uses). Sad when the buildings completely disappear." . . . "That was my school from 2nd grade. What a wonderful school. So sorry to read this. I remember Miss Grinvalsky, Miss Heffernan, Mr. Fox, and my favorite Mrs. Risley who gave me my love of history." . . . "Seeing these destruction pictures make me sad and at the same time happy because of the wonderful memories!"

Post: Sledding In Torrington

The below image was on the Christmas Party invitation sent out recently by the Torrington Historical Society. The back of the postcard states that the boy in the photo is unidentified, the photo itself is circa 1920s, and that the winter moment was snapped on Cooper Street, which is behind Southwest School. . . Love the photo. And love remembrances of winter sledding past. When I was young, the neighborhood kids used to sled on the hill behind Billy White's house on Four Story Lane. It looked like a mountain to us little tykes. Later, with my own sons, the Bentleys were very fond of the steep hill at West Torrington. We still have the toboggan we used there.

(Photo: Collection of the Torrington Historical Society.)

Responses included: "One clue to who the child in the picture might be is that I know that a nearby house was built by Mr. Maigret (I forget his first name). He built it himself and raised his family there. Then the Cardillos owned it. If anybody knows any of the Maigret or Cardillo descendants/relatives, they may know if the child is from one of those families, or whose family he's from. Admittedly, it was a long time ago, *but* someone might know." . . . "Ahh, the good old days before street salt was used. We'd have sledding on the streets for days after a storm, and we had some major hills in our neighborhood. My 1955 Flexible Flyer is still hung up in the garage." . . . "Yes, before road salt and sand ruined all the fun. We used to sled the length of Cole Street, a rather steep and long run, which intersected at the bottom with Ricciardone Avenue, a busy street. For the last 100 yards we had to turn our sleds sideways and skid a long way to stop before shooting out onto Ricciardone and potentially being run over. Never a fear in any of us." . . . "We spent many a winter day at the hill in West Torrington. It was a five minute walk. Especially liked it when the hill was cleared farther up and the rope tow was added."

(Above, looking down from the top of the hill at West Torrington circa 1980s. That's Riverside Avenue at the bottom and the garages of Turri Electric. A sledder with a "Flying Saucer" can be seen in the foreground, and the old upright supports for the tow rope can barely be seen mid-picture on the left.)

. . . "I remember going to West Torrington too. It was a long walk up, but the tow rope helped a lot. It was one steep hill." . . . "I spent countless hours sledding at West Torrington as well as the Torrington Country Club with friends and family. Great memories!" . . ."West Torrington - that hill! It was something when I was in 6th,7th, and 8th grade. The only issue was how to ride the sled: stomach down or sitting. Fortunately I never had an accident, but there was this feeling when you hit the bottom and looked up to the top and knew you had the whole afternoon to do it again. Great memory." . . . "Sledding at West Torrington was a very big treat. Our parents had to drop us. We used my Grandfather's toboggan and all the young members of my family were aboard. Fond memories!" . . . "December of 1969 or '70, while home from college for Christmas, I rode a sled from the top of the West Torrington ski slope. A great ride till I reached the bottom where the sled dug in and I didn't. I went head first into the packed run-out and snapped my collar bone. Had it set at Charlotte Hungerford and went back to college wearing a bra-like canvas harness to keep the bone in place. I took it off four weeks later and never went back to a doctor to have it checked out. At four weeks, if I moved too quickly I could feel the still-mending bone bend a bit." . . . "Had many toboggan rides down West Torrington. The goal was always to try and reach the road (Riverside Avenue) at the end of the slide."

(Above, the bottom of the hill at West Torrington, circa 1980s. The ride down was always exhilarating, the walk back up exhausting.)

. . . "We would go to West Torrington when we lived on Clark Street, but once we moved to Litchfield Street, we would sled on the vacant lot across the street owned by the Booth family. Now, unfortunately, it is the site of an assisted living facility (Keystone)." . . . "We used to slide down the steep street just around the corner from our house on Clark. We'd station someone at the bottom of the hill to warn us about approaching cars. In the summer we used that same hill for our 'soap box' cars, but for some reason we used the sidewalk instead of the road!" . . . "We used to sled for hours down McKinley Street. We walked all the way to the top where Joanne and Shiela Ingoldsby lived and the Giarneses. Then went all the way down all 3 sections of the hill to the bottom where Mary Ann Considine lived. Then we trudged back up the hill and did it again. It was worth every step!" . . . "Believe it or not, I have a very early memory of sledding down Highland Avenue. We would walk up, sled down, and make a turn onto Workman Avenue. Not something I would do today, but back then traffic was different. Once we moved to the East Side of town, we would go down Sunrise Drive, the road we lived on. It was a great little hill and again had little traffic." . . . "I lived on Holly Place on the West Side, and we slid down Guilford Street. Guilford was the place to be after a snowstorm! It had less traffic than Highland. The city even had a police officer there for safety." . . . "I would go visit Joe Petrovits on Elmwood Terrace and take my sled. I could slide all the way home to Bannon Street and have to walk only a couple of short distances." . . . "My father would take us to West Torrington for hours of sledding. Didn't appreciate then the hours he spent waiting for us. Thanks Dad!" . . . "Wish we had those inflatable snow tubes back then." . . . "Still have my original American Flyer. The best Christmas gift ever!"

(Right, the Bentley toboggan, still in nice condition, stands upright ready for action. This toboggan was purchased at Stars in the mid-1980s, and saw a lot of West Torrington sledding back in those years.)

Post: Torrington Circuses - Under The Big Top

August 1929, 90+ years ago, the circus came to town. Although most circus troupes have long since gone the way of the Model-T, ninety years ago it was *still* a big deal, a carryover from the pre-movie, pre-radio, pre-nothing-to-do-in-this-one-horse-town days. There'd be advanced advertising in the local newspaper, flyers put up, and when the circus arrived, usually by train, there would be a parade through town. . . In mid-August 1929, readers of *The Torrington Register* began seeing display ads for the upcoming Christy Brothers circus. The ads promised a "mammoth," 5-ring show comprised of 500 horses; 50 cages of animals to include lions, elephants, and camels; all lit by 2 complete electric light systems, and supported by 5 bands, 2 calliopes, and 1250 performers (clowns, dancing girls, aerialists, et al), roustabouts, etc. There would be a "1000 Character Bible Spectacle - Noah and the Ark" and Christy Bros. billed themselves as "The Longest, Costliest, and Most Magnificent." In the "old" days, prior to 1929, when the circus hit town there was always a street parade. There would be a long line of wagons, performers, cages, etc.

(Above, one wagon of a circus parade on Torrington's Main Street, circa early 20th century. Trolley tracks can be seen in the dirt thoroughfare. The W.W. Mertz Company is directly behind the horses, and the Odd Fellows [I.O.O.F.] hall is to the right of that on the upper stories. An early automobile and cyclist appear to be keeping pace with the horse-drawn wagon. Circus parades were generally spread out, especially the multiple bands, to stretch out the enjoyment. Photo compliments of Robert Britton.)

that would negotiate the main thoroughfare. Locals would line the streets and excitement would build. However, in 1929 most circuses had given up performing street parades with the rare exception of the Christy Bros. It was said the owner and manager, G.W. Christy, was a circus veteran, "born and reared under the flapping canvas walls of a circus tent" and that "he contends that circus day without a parade is cheating the youngsters out of one of their unalienable rights.". . On Saturday, August 24, 1929, at 6:50 a.m. twenty big railroad cars arrived at the Torrington depot on Water Street. Throughout the morning large circus wagons rumbled between the depot and the parade grounds on the Stefurak Lot on East Elm, a.k.a. Steffy's Lot. NOTE: This lot would later be home to the Litchfield Farm Shop, and today is the site of the Torrington Post Office. . . The tents went up and by noon the parade started. It normally would have gone

(Above, the Christy Brothers circus parade in 1929 on lower East Main at the intersection with Main. Many horses and a couple of carriages can be seen. The spectators are crowding in very close, narrowing the street. The large elms that once graced the downtown area are clearly visible.)

down the length of Main, but Main Street was torn up for street paving, so the circus parade had to follow "a rather devious line," which had been worked out between the Torrington chief of police and a circus representative. The route included East Main. There were 2 shows that August day: 2 and 8 p.m. Customers were allowed to enter an hour early, and though no account exists of the actual shows, there's little doubt that Torringtonians turned out in force and filled the tents for both shows, as was customary.

(Above, the Christy Bros. circus set up in Steffy's Lot on East Elm in 1929. View is looking across East Elm from Brook Street. On the far left a blurred auto can be seen speeding into the scene. In the lower left, the top of a car is barely visible. The main entrance to the Big Top can be seen straight ahead, slightly to the left of center.)

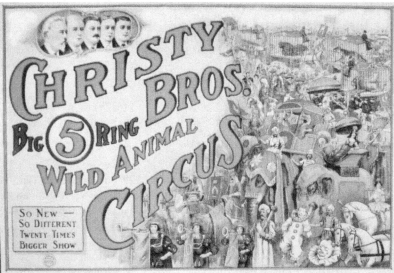

(Above, an original Christy Brothers poster circa 1920s.)

. . . In the years before 1929, though circuses had been an integral part of entertainment in Torrington, they'd set up at different locations and not on Steffy's Lot. A popular location prior to 1901 was a patch of open land around where Center and Franklin Streets are today, i.e. between the river and East Main. After 1901, when streets and houses were put into that tract, the premier circus location was League Park, today Fuessenich Park. Eventually it was felt though that the circus made too much of a mess of the baseball/ football fields, so between 1910 and 1921, circuses set up at Murphy's Park, a.k.a. The Torrington Riding Park far down the South End where the sewage plant is today. This is the same site where the black 10th Cavalry encamped in August 1912 (see my book *The Twilight Of Torrington Days*). After the Christy Brothers used Stefurak's Lot in 1929, a popular location became Hendey's Lot, on the corner of Park Avenue and East Albert Streets. Though this lot was long and narrow, it was just big enough to accommodate most shows. Today it's home to the Sullivan Senior Center. In later years a vacant lot on Oak Avenue was used, though it was reported that the power lines over the back of the property were a detriment. . . I have no memory of ever attending a major circus in Torrington. I fondly remember some small circuses/carnivals, especially one on the Winsted Road. . . On one hand it's sad to think the day of the circus has come-and-gone for the most part. *But*, for many years in Torrington, they furnished a valuable part of local entertainment *and* the expansion of life in general. For not much money, locals could be transported to worlds far beyond our valley, stimulate their senses and imagination, and literally broaden their horizons.

Responses included: "I do recall attending a circus in Torrington when I was 5 or 6-years-old. I remember a clown shooting a faux gun and the sound scared the poop out of me. I fell through the bleachers. Luckily my mother caught me by the arm so I didn't fall all the way down. That was my last circus." . . . "I remember carnivals coming - late 40s-early 50s - to Fuessenich Park or an area nearby. The main attractions for me were the rides which were both scary and exciting." . . . "I have vague memories of a circus that my mom took me to when I was very young. The venue was in the South End." . . . "I always attended the circus at Hendey's Lot in my younger years. The 1955 Flood washed out some of the lot and when the Naugatuck River was widened for flood control, the lot became too small for a circus. I don't remember a circus coming to town after 1955." . . . "Yes, I remember going to the circus in the 1950s. I think it was down near Tavano Glass Company." . . . "I remember my mother talking about a circus coming to Torrington (she would have been 9 or 10-years-old), and I do believe she commented on the animals being led through the streets. As I recall, she talked of the circus locating in the South end of town." . . . "I remember the carnivals that were held up in the Stars parking lot. In fact, I got stuck for over an hour right at the top of the Ferris wheel." . . . "I remember those Stars' carnivals. That was the last Ferris wheel I have been on. It was so rickety I thought I was going to fall off!" . . .

(Left, an undated cardboard poster advertising a Winsted Road circus. The colors are red, white, and blue.)

"As a teen about 1964, I attended a carnival in the new plaza we called the Bradlees Plaza. I met a cute girl there, and we went on a fun ride that whipped us around. All of a sudden, she said, 'Uh-oh!' I asked what was wrong. 'My bra strap broke,' she said. What does a gentleman do when that happens?"

(Above, a circus wagon turns in the center of Torrington's Main Street, early in the 1900s. To the right would be Center Bridge. Franklin Street and the river would be dead ahead, and East Main to the left. Note once again, the trolley tracks in the dirt street. Note also the dogs on top of the wagon, and the automobile on the far right. It was an age of transition. Photo compliments of Robert Britton.)

Post: Strike Up The Crops - A 1929 Musical Weekend

One of my favorite pieces of Torrington memorabilia is a 2-sided, canvas banner from 1929. (See opposite page.) It's large, approximately 12'x5', and hangs in my basement. It's beige with navy blue lettering, and though stained and ripped, is handsome and represents a remarkable part of Torrington history. I can say with 99% certainty it was done by Torrington sign painter Charles Harris, who did MANY banners of this sort back in the early 20th century, and I've seen several others, though I passed on buying them.

(Above, a Charles Harris banner hanging up in the rafters of a Litchfield County antique store, a banner I didn't buy. This one is circa 1920s and is advertising a "SPRING FESTIVAL" at the Palace Theatre in Torrington. Note: The Palace Theatre was built in 1920, which predates the Warner in Torrington by slightly over a decade. In the early years, it was always billed as the "Warner Bros Palace," presumably because the Warner Brothers owned it.)

. . . Sidebar: Charles Harris (1876-1932) was born in Mechanic Falls, Maine, and moved to Torrington in 1912. He purchased a local sign painting business, expanded it, and renamed it the Harris Advertising Business. It was located at various locations throughout town, most notably on lower East Main. When he died in 1932, his wife Annie sold the business to Frederic Short who operated the business until his own death in 1972. . . The canvas is heavy and well stitched. Note the wind hole sewn into the center. This banner, undoubtedly, hung outside and saw a LOT of Torrington weather

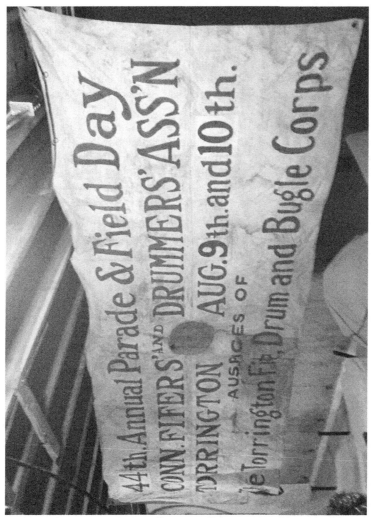

over the years. I say "over the years" because although this event happened in 1929, the banner, without question, was used before that. Torrington also hosted the annual Fifers and Drummers event in 1921 AND 1915. Note that the "44," "9," and "10" are sewn-on patches, i.e. this banner was used before and most likely it was used in both 1921 and 1915. To find out, however, what number is painted on the original canvas, I'd have to undo at least some of the stitches on the "44" and I don't want to do that. . . In any case, let's flashback to that long ago August 1929 weekend and a Torrington of flappers and Model Ts. It was a weekend that spotlighted the Torrington Fife,

Drum, and Bugle Corps, a group that had first formed back in 1913 as a fife and drum corps. Its first roster consisted of 18 musicians. The following year, 8 buglers were added, and the now fife, drum, *and* bugle corps took 1st prize in the State Convention in Middletown, i.e. they were the champions of Connecticut! In 1915 the Torrington Corps hosted the parade and field in Torrington with 40 corps in attendance, and hosted again in 1921 with 52 corps present. In 1917 theTorrington Fife, Drum, and Bugle Corps won the championship of the United States at Newburgh, NY, competing against 27 other corps from 7 states. . . In the first World War, seventeen members served in the Armed Forces; one member was killed and two were wounded. From 1913-1929 the Torrington Corps paraded and played on 244 different occasions, marched over 2000 miles, traveled approximately 7000 miles, and won 197 prizes including Silver Loving Cups *and* gold and silver medals for individual and group competition. The Torrington Corps had a proud and accomplished history by the time it hosted the August 1929 state-wide event. . .

(Left, a very worn souvenir pinback and ribbon from the August 1929 competition. The pinback has a picture of the Torrington Fife, Drum, and Bugle Corps, and the ribbon says, "44th Annual Parade & Field Day Exercises. Connecticut Fifers & Drummers Association. Torrington, CT. Aug. 10, 1929)

The preparation to host the many musical corps from all over the state involved considerable months of preparation, as well as many volunteers and sponsors. A very few of the Torringtonians who helped in the organization included Bernard Dahlen who had been Secretary-Treasurer of the State Association for the last 7 years and had been a member of the Torrington Corps since its founding in 1913.

(Right, a dapper Bernard Dahlen in 1929.)

John J. Smedick who, though retired from active competition himself, had won 67 prizes for Baton Swinging in the last 15 years. Lieutenant Colonel Ernest Novey who functioned as the Grand Marshal. Local judges included Mayor Charles Newcomb and Torrington City Council members Erwin Manteuffel, William A. Gleeson, et al. . .

(Right, a high-collared William Gleeson. He was on the Torrington City Council at this time, while in his professional life he owned the very successful Gleeson Mortuary on Prospect Street.)

The big weekend started with all groups as they arrived in town checking in at the Torrington Corps headquarters on Franklin Street. It stayed open all Friday night and served hot coffee and sandwiches. Next came a street parade, which left the Armory at 8 p.m. and proceeded over the main downtown streets. It involved all the corps which arrived on time. Not all did. For example, a featured group was the 71st Regiment Field Music out of NYC. They didn't arrive until 1 a.m. and were quartered at the YMCA. Approximately 42 groups did arrive on time and marched. A "Hickville clown parade," put on by the Lancroft Corps of New Haven, followed at around 10 p.m. Then, a ball was held at the Armory, which also involved baton swinging and fancy drilling contests. . . The main competitions were Saturday at Fuessenich Park, but due to rain had to move indoors at the Armory. A total of 46 groups competed, in addition to 3 incomplete delegations from other corps, making a total of 49 groups represented. Torrington restauranteurs Sabotka and Alicky were in charge of lunch, and they served approximately 1500 uniformed participants. It was reported that it was one of *the* most successful corps weekends the state had ever seen. Though many group and individual prizes were awarded, there was no mention of anyone from the Torrington contingent winning anything. Were they allowed

(Above, members of the Torrington Fife, Drum, & Bugle Corps pose
for a picture with some of their many previously won trophies.)

to compete? Did they have to recluse themselves because of being the host city and furnishing many of the judges? There was no mention in the newspaper accounts regarding this. BUT, for certain, it was *still* a grand weekend, one that few would ever forget.

200

Responses included: "I can imagine the anticipation and excitement throughout Torrington and the surrounding area. It must have been quite an event. Thanks for posting all this!" . . . "That banner is an amazing piece of history!" . . . "Interesting. The history of more recent fife and drum corps had their genesis after the return of service men from WWII." . . . "I saw another Torrington group, The John Brown Ancients, once in what they called a Muster in Chester, Connecticut. There were fife and drum bands from as far away as Ft. Lauderdale. It was a 3 hour parade. My wife, my daughter, and I cheered for each band."

(Above top, a vintage aluminum car badge from the aforementioned John Brown Ancients. . .   Above bottom, a vintage license plate/ license plate topper. Note: The Vagabonds, and other later Torrington drum and bugle corps were direct descendants of the 1913 Torrington Fife, Drum & Bugle Corps.)

Post: Driver's Education - Proceed With Caution

Late March 1957. The driver's ed program at THS got a new car from Zele Chevrolet. It was a little late for the seniors in the Class Of 1957, but the underclassmen would be learning to drive in style.

(Above, a rather rough quality newspaper clipping from late March 1957. Photo credit to James Miller. L-R: Driver instructor Frank Faita, Principal Richard Williamson, Richard Zele of Zele Chevrolet Co. Richard Zele is handing over the keys to a new car to THS Principal Williamson, while future student trainees crowd the high school steps looking on.)

I note that Frank Faita, even back then, was a driving instructor. I took my lessons from him in spring 1964, and at that time he had his own business (Faita A-C School Of Driving) at 160 Torrington Heights Road, though I believe he was still associated with the Torrington High program as an instructor. . . Frank Faita was a good guy: even tempered, not prone to panic. I certainly put him to the test one Thursday evening. Traffic was heavy. We approached the North End rotary going north on Main. Traffic was merging from the right (East Elm) and had the right-of-way. BUT, I didn't want to slow down and have to shift. The car was a Falcon Sprint, 4-on-the-floor, and shifting for a brand new driver like me was tough, or at least a trial. Rather than hit the brakes and have to downshift, I hit the gas and roared into the rotary. Mr. Faita hit his own set of brakes, and we came to a virtual stop. He looked like he was in shock, a bit ashen; I'm not sure if he was sweating. He turned to me, told me to slow down, and I eased the car forward and did. The rest of the drive was uneventful. I'm not sure how old he was when he died, but if Mr. Faita had any more students like me, it certainly had to have hastened his demise. . . Who was your own driving instructor? Any anecdotes you'd care to share?

(Above, Frank Faita in 1964. He was a man of even temperament and great composure, not easily rattled by student drivers who could scarcely start a car, much less navigate traffic.)

Responses included: "Mr. Faita was also my driving instructor and almost the same event happened with me in Waterbury." . . . "I had Doc Sacco for a driving instructor. I can't remember any great driving adventures like yours. He had automatic transmissions. I believe he was weak in his training in backing up. To this day I'm weak at that. I can parallel park, but I try not to. My early cars didn't

have power steering, so turning the wheel a lot wasn't easy. I failed the test the first time for backing up. The second time I had Jutso Carbone. He was a great guy, and he was from my mother's Italian neighborhood. He had me back into his driveway, and I passed." . . . "I had Frank Faita for THS Driver's Ed in late 1965-early '66. I believe the only option with him was to learn on an automatic transmission. At the same time my mother was teaching me the manual shift at Hillside Cemetery. There were a few instances of my stopping the car, getting out and slamming the door, while she slid over and took the wheel and I got in on the passenger side. That'd be the end of the lesson for that day. Silent ride home. To this day I often think of Mr. Faita when I parallel park, as he taught that skill very effectively. It served me particularly well in the years I lived in big cities." . . .

(Left, a souvenir pencil from the 1960s. The first line says, "TEENAGE DRIVER EDUCATION." The second states, "FAITA DRIVING SCHOOL."

"I learned to drive a manual car in February when I was 16. Mr. Faita's assistant had me parallel park on Church Street that had a slight incline. After many tries I managed to squeeze into a space but was sweating up a storm. For years I avoided parallel parking, even with an automatic transmission!" . . . "I remember going to class at Mr. Faita's house. Small room with lots of kids." . . . "I also went to class at Faita's house. The school classes were always full. My starkest memory was of the films showing accidents! I have no idea what kind of car I drove with him.

Seems to be the men who remember that. My dad taught me to drive a stick shift, and I drove them for years. I had a 5-speed Honda Prelude in the 1980s that I loved but injured my right shoulder and after surgery ended up having to get rid of it because it hurt so much. Loved that car."

(Above, the former Frank Faita home at 160 Torrington Heights Road in 2015. It looked pretty much the same as this back when most student drivers attended classes here in the 1950s-'70s as part of the "Faita A-C School of Driving." Classes were held in that small porch-like addition on the right.)

. . . "I STILL have scary memories of those films." . . . "I took lessons from Mr Faita and thought he was the kindest man. Cool as a cucumber." . . . "I also attended school at Faita's on Torrington Heights Road. Because my brother had already taught me how to drive, Mr. Faita had me drive to Hartford and back to get my hours in. Hahaha." . . . "I too attended Faita's Driving School. My grandpa used to let me drive his truck in the fields in the back of his house. I was fairly young, maybe 12, when I learned how to drive the truck. So much fun." . . . "I learned to drive on a Chevy station wagon with 3-on-the-column. A test from Dad was to start at the slight incline at the stop sign on Broad Street without rolling back. Those were, and will always be, good memories. Had numerous standard cars through the years. Guess if I had to I could still drive a standard. Definitely no hills where I live now." . . . "I too learned at Faita's A-C School Of Driving in 1964. I don't think that I put him through any memorable moments though." . . . "I was a Faita grad. Nightmares from the accident films. One of the films was of a truck accident. Single vehicle event. The truck bed was loaded with large metal pipes. When the truck struck a barrier all those pipes moved forward and crushed the cab. Now I don't follow trucks with pipes. I can still see those images today. Maybe that's why I watch YouTube videos of Russian car accidents recorded on dash cams? BTW: Mr. Faita slept in the passenger seat while I drove to Watertown and back to get the miles in. At NIGHT!" . . . "The research on that scary movie tactic reveals that it is *not* effective regardless of whatever behavior you are trying to influence (i. e. scare)." . . . "I took his classes also, for insurance purposes if I remember correctly. You got a lower rate after passing his course." . . . "I had Doc Sacco because he was a friend of my father's." . . . "I had Mr Faita. Learned to drive in a Nash Rambler, I believe. Stick on the column. Most trying lesson: stopping on a hill and starting up again without sliding back. Required coordinated brake, clutch, and accelerator work." . . . "That's why in the old days we always gave the car ahead of us stopped at a light on a hill PLENTY of room, i.e. the slide back factor." . . . "Funny story about mom teaching me to drive. I was driving my mom's '54 Chevy, turquoise-and-white. My Dad had the 'newer car' - a 1955 Buick in baby blue. We went to Doyles Drug Store, and I pulled between 2 cars nicely, went in, and did an errand. Upon returning, I got back in the driver's seat and proceeded to back up, turning the wheel to angle the car out around the rear ends of the cars beside me for a 'first.' Not watching the front of the car, I sideswiped the car on my right in doing so. Oops! Immediately my mother yelled, 'Get out of the car, quick!' We both got out, me not knowing what was happening. She told me to get in the passenger seat, which I did while she went back in the store, found the owner and took the blame. Wow. Never saw her take the blame for anything I did! Later she told me if I took the blame, we'd lose the Learner's Permit, and it would be a long time before I got my license. Thanks Mom!" . . . "I had Mr. Faita at THS. Most memorable event was with a fellow student in the parking lot at Doyle's Drug Store. I was in the back seat. Car was facing a stone wall. Instead of putting the car in reverse, she put it in drive. Thank goodness for dual brakes!" . . . "Mr. Faita was my driving instructor back in 1956! My dad also took me out to practice hilltop stops and then restarts; very scary and frustrating on standard transmission cars!" . . . "I took from Faita's A-C School Of Driving in 1963. He was very patient."

(Above, student drivers with Frank Faita in 1966. Behind the steering wheel is Jim Pavlicovic. Melanie Dreisbach is on the left in the backseat, and Alberta Volpe is on the right. The car itself is a Ford Mustang. Frank Faita always had hot cars available for teen trainees, which undoubtedly helped maintain a strong attraction for his school. Note the license plate and the "FAITA SCHOOL OF DRIVING" placard above it. There could be no doubt who owned this car, as it frequently cruised Torrington streets. It was a great advertising strategy.)

Post: The Cavallari Post

The John Cavallari Post #11 was a Torrington, Italian-American veterans' organization that was founded in 1937 by 6 veterans of WWI. The post was named after Giovanni "John" Cavallari, the first American soldier from Torrington of Italian heritage to die in WWI. Private Cavallari was serving with the Torrington unit - Company M,

102nd Infantry - when he was killed. He was a member of Sergeant (later General) Ernest Novey's platoon.

(Left, an undated photo of the WWI doughboy, Private Giovanni "John" Cavallari in his uniform with tie and campaign hat.)

From its founding in 1937 to the years immediately following WWII, The Post's membership rose rapidly. Around 1946, members bought a home at 57 Migeon Avenue. The beautiful house was set back, and was sited behind where the Oldsmobile dealership was; today it's the Honda dealership. On the first floor was a large assembly hall. The second floor held a library, a meeting hall, and the office of the Post's Ladies' Auxiliary. In the basement was a tap room and cocktail lounge.

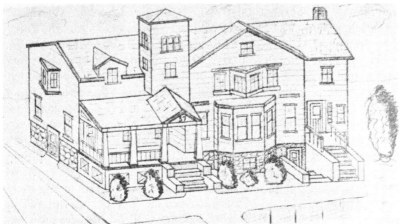

(Above, a drawing of the front of The Cavallari Post, circa 1946, artist unknown. It could have rightly been considered a mini-mansion, a very prestigious edifice. . . Below, Cornelio Oldsmobile Motor Sales [today the Honda dealership] on Migeon Avenue, circa early 1970s. The Cavallari Post was behind this and to the right.)

Perhaps some of you visited The Post, were members, or remember some of the events it sponsored. It hosted fundraising dinners in which celebrities were the guest speakers. It marched in the Memorial Day Parade, took part in the November Armistice Day ceremony, helped to organize the creation of the Christopher Columbus Statue/Memorial just off East Main (dedicated October 12, 1980), etc. It had the best lodge headquarters of any of the local veteran groups (VFW, American Legion Post 38, Catholic War

Veterans - St. Francis Post No. 1086, Jewish War Veterans - Litchfield County No. 294,, DeMartino Tedesco Post No. 16, Polish War Veterans - Alex T. Kaczmarczyk Post, Daughters Of the American Revolution, etc.), and it had a large roster of well known Torrington names. For example, in 1965 its membership included: Joe Barrante, Renny Belli, Aldo Bergonzi, Jim Bruni, Frank Buonocore, Nick Caputi, Louie Carillo, Ray Carmignani, Joe Cianciolo, Joe DiPippo, Al Gaioni, Anthony Gelormino, Tom Grieco, Nick Infante, Tom LaPorta, Ralph Leone, Dante Longobucco, Vinnie Martinotti, Larry Mencuccini, John Minetto, Ray Oneglia, Anthony Pasquariello, John Pergola, Vic Reis, Stephen Rolli, Frank Russo, John Speziale, Lou Strano, Primo Zanderigo, and so many, *many* more. These were very well known people, *and* The Cavallari Post was the most high profile post in its day. . . Please feel free to share any memories you have of this fraternal group and/or its members. Sad to say, very few of these veterans are still alive today.

Responses included: "So many familiar names, including my uncle, Stephen Rolli. The Italians had a strong influence in Torrington's development, especially in the first half of the last century." . . . "To encourage members to march in the Memorial Day Parade, my father, who was a member, served a pasta dinner (what else?) at the club, and we'd spend the day there. The day before we went to the cemetery decorating graves."

(Above, a car carrying Cavallari Post veterans too infirm to walk the Memorial Day Parade route passes through the center of town in 1986. The banner on the side says, "JOHN CAVALLARI POST 11, I.A.W.V." The latter standing for Italian American War Veterans. Photo: Collection of the Torrington Historical Society.)

. . . "Tessie Martinotti made a mini-uniform for my brother to wear when he marched with our dad." . . . "One vivid memory I have was the crack of bocce balls hitting each other during the summer months. And well into the evening! Our backyard on Hotchkiss Place abutted the court." . . . "I was dragged to a lot of weddings there when I was a pup. Usually I spent the whole time out in back watching all the old Italian guys playing bocce. They treated me great. Played a few gigs there with my band in later years. It was a nice building. I knew a lot of the members that you listed." . . . "Though it's not The Cavallari Post, I went to several weddings as a kid at the Knights of Columbus, another Italian group. I remember running back and forth to the bar to get ginger ales with cherries. I loved watching my Italian grandmother dance the tarantella with family and friends." . . . "So many familiar names, and at a time when I think Torrington was about 60% Italian. I love it!"

(Above, members are gathered in the Assembly Hall of The Cavallari Post on Migeon Avenue to hear featured speaker Andy Robustelli, who's at the microphone. Robustelli was not only a star on the New York Giants, but was also an Italian-American. Note the "WELCOME Andy" banner behind him and the film projector being set up on the left. No doubt that NY Giants film highlights were shown. Photo: Collection of the Torrington Historical Society.)

Post: The Soap Box Derby - When Gravity Rules

Hell On Wheels. Wooden Streaks Of Lightning. Do you remember when Torrington had Soap Box Derby competition on East Main *or* Kinney Street? Homemade "soapboxes" streaking down the hill, viewers lining both sides of the street. . . From 1958-1960 (3 years), the course for the Torrington Soap Box Derby went down East Main. In those early years excitement was great. Although the All-American Soap Box Derby had annually been held in Akron, Ohio, since 1934 and drew national media attention, Torrington had never held a race. All that changed in 1958.

(Left, a souvenir pinback from the 1958 Torrington race.)

The Torrington Jaycees were in charge. They oversaw the pre-race preparation *and* the race day competition. PRE-RACE: Would-be racers picked up their wheels, tires, and axles from race headquarters, i.e. everyone raced with those same components. There were also detailed instructions regarding the physical makeup of the car. For example, the total weight of the racer and driver could not exceed 250 pounds. The brake had to be a single drag system. The overall length could not exceed 80 inches. And more. The instructions were all very intimidating for the average youngster. A big rule was that the "soap box" itself had to be built entirely by the entrant. Adults could "advise and counsel," but that was *it*! Undoubtedly this latter rule was the one most frequently violated. For example, in 1958 I vividly recall visiting a would-be Derby-ist in my neighborhood in the months leading up to race day. I was with a couple of other kids, and we wanted the boy to "come out and play." When we saw he was busy with his car (actually standing next to it in the garage watching his father do the work), I said something like, You're busy. We'll catch you some other time. He replied along the lines of, Let's go. This is my father's project. Sidebar: AND, it *was*. . . The 1958 race was held on that most patriotic of days, the Fourth of July. The course started from around where the New Harwinton Road (Rt.4) forks off, down to above where Burger King/Route 8 is today. There was no Route 8 to pass under (the "new" Route 8 hadn't been built yet), East School was still on East Main (today the "glass building"), and Hillside Pharmacy still dominated the fork-in-the-road where East Elm branches off from East Main. This was a bit below where the finish line actually was. Approximately 50 youngsters had entered, and the festivities began with a parade of the competitors marching in uniform (t-shirt and helmet) over Willow Street and right onto East Main.

(Above, Willow Street; July 4, 1958. The competitors march in "files-on-parade" behind a flatbed truck carrying a band. Photo: Collection of the Torrington Historical Society.)

East Main had been divided into 3 lanes, and a racer had to stay in the lane assigned or be disqualified. A couple ultimately were. There were two age groups: Class A (13-15) and Class B (11-12). In the preliminary heats, racers competed against those of their own age group. Once a winner was decided in each of the two classes, those 2 division champions raced in the finals to determine the city champion. This "final," was a single race, winner-take-all, no 2-out-of-3 or any other determining measure. It put a lot of pressure on the finalist, especially considering all the work which had gone into the soap box construction (typically around 100 hours) and all the problems which had to be overcome, e.g. keeping total cost under

$25 (an itemized cost list had to be submitted), keeping the weight under 250 pounds when the racer himself/herself was in a growing spurt, developing a brake and steering system that worked, etc. . . For the 1958 Torrington race, and the local races which followed in later years, traffic on East Main was detoured. Five thousand spectators lined the hill. The finish line judges were Renny Belli, Dennis Brennan, William DeMichiel, and Joseph Lucas, i.e. winners were determined strictly by the human eye. There was no electronic timing or finish line sensors in 1958. . . Things got rolling with a special novelty race featuring Mayor Anthony Gelormino (on the left in the below picture), Edmund Waller from WTOR (in the middle), and Richard Zele of Zele Chevrolet (on the far right). I remember as

(Above, the novelty race, adult contestants in 1958 charge down East Main, about 25-feet from the start. Richard Zele on the right, driving his car named "Lazy Suzy," won. Note the slightly inclined, starting ramps behind them and the crowd of amused onlookers. Route 4, a.k.a. the New Harwinton Road forks off to the right of this. Photo: Collection of the Torrington Historical Society.)

a curious 10-year-old walking up to the above starting line and checking things out. My overwhelming impression was how well organized everything was. Race officials wore white pith helmets and kept things running smoothly. The races went off without a hitch, and first heat winners were Edward Gallo, Jim Kahn, Dave Iffland, Frank McCann, Tom Hayes, Jerry Ringsted, Tommy Zampini, Dave Blakeslee, Jerry Zawadzkas, Bernie Mucci, Raymond Signorelli, Dave Wilson, Richard Wadhams, and Gary Cicognani. Succeeding heats wilted the contestants down even more until there were 2 divi-

(Above, two 1958 entrants are caught in the exact moment that the front of the starting ramp has gone down. Sponsors' names can be seen on the sides of the cars. Photo: Collection of the Torrington Historical Society. . . Below, an official t-shirt that all the Torrington racers wore.)

sion champions: 13-year-old Edward Gallo in Class A and 12-year-old Tommy Zampini in Class B. The 1958 finals featured these two boys, and the 5000 fans could not have been treated to a more exciting finish to the city's first Derby day. After head starter John Bickford fired the gun, the boys rolled down the 1000 foot, East Main course nose-to-nose, until Tom Zampini edged ahead and won the close race. . .

(Above, Tom Zampini crosses the finish line, edging out Edward Gallo. View is looking up East Main. This section of the street has totally changed in the last 61 years. . . Below, Tommy Zampini poses with his racer and trophy. Both Photos: Collection of the Torrington Historical Society.)

1958 Postscript: Tommy Zampini went to The Nationals, a.k.a. the All American Soap Box Derby at Derby Downs in Akron, Ohio, but unfortunately was beaten by around 7 car lengths in the first heat by Freddie Foster of Charlotte, NC and 2 car lengths by Jim Saul of New Orleans, LA. Still, Tom Zampini was Torrington's first ever soap box winner, and that is *quite* a distinction. . . As great a race day as 1958 was, 1959 was even better. More fans turned out (around 8000), more racers competed, the final finish was even closer, and race sponsor WTOR broad-casted the entire race start-to-finish.

(Right, a 1959 souvenir pinback with "WTOR," Torrington's one-and-only radio station, proudly displayed.)

Raymond Avenia was the race day chairman and the following served as judges: Robert Kelly, Maurice Hoben, and Frank Cimino. Other Derby officials included track director Addo Bonetti, director of hill top operations Roosevelt Perry Jr., finish line director Joseph Speetjens, chief starter Tom DiVita, registrar Pat Pioppi, clerk of the course William D'Aquilla, chief inspector Angelo Lampanaro, public address announcer Muff Maskowsky, and general director Robert Massut. Pre-race instructions to spectators reiterated they should stay on the sidewalks at all times and that they were requested *not* to cross the street at any time during a race. Because there was no parking on any of the streets leading to the East Main portion of the track site, Haydon Manufacturing on East Elm (today's new Vinnie's) offered free usage of their parking lot to race goers. Vending of any kind was prohibited except by those properly licensed and those permanent businesses on East Main. Again, the day started with a parade of the contestants, and again the race heats rolled by uninterrupted except for one incident. A car in Lane 1 driven by Richard Johnstone crashed into the crowd just south of the East Elm-East Main intersection. Johnstone reported that his goggles had become fogged up on his way down the hill and that he was unable to see. A doctor reported that the young boy was fine except for a slight lip injury. First heat winners in 1959 included Edward Gallo, Raymond Signorelli, Peter O'Connor, Porter Harvey Jr., Jim Kahn, Wayne Arnold, Gerry Zawadzkas, Tony Pasquariello, Gary Cicognani, Gary Arnold, Frank Faita Jr., Carl Muller, Albert Gallo, John Kelmelis, Dave Wilson, Tom Petrovits, Tom Bruni, and T. Knapp. The closest and *the* most important heat occurred in the second round when Jim Kahn and Edward Gallo finished in a dead heat. A run-off was declared, and in the re-match Gallo beat Kahn "by a scant six-inch margin." Those 6 inches, unfortunately for Kahn, cost him the Torrington championship and a trip to Akron because Edward Gallo went on to win the city championship when he beat his brother, the younger Albert, in the finals. Historic Sidebar: In competing against each other in the finals, the Gallo boys became the first ever brother combination in National Soap Box Derby history to finish 1-2. Ultimately then, what was a tough break for Jim Kahn in the run-off became a moment of national derby prominence. . . On June 6, 1960, the third Derby was held. Raymond Avenia was the general chairman, and a host of young competitors raced for the gold. Entrants were a combination of race veterans and rookies. Among those who competed were Richard Acheson, Al Columbia, William Smyth, Don Ponak, Bruce Murphy, Jim Juhas, Don LaRocco, Denis Borra, Bill Post, Tom "Gas" Petrovits, Albert Gallo, Mike Boyle, Bill Russell, Richard Dagenais, Lance Watts, Floyd Amicone, Robert Nicholas, Bruce Wilber, Leonard "Skip" Day, Louis Bennett, Roger Richard, Carl Muller, Frank Faita Jr., Edward Poucher, Ernest Elliott, Cliff Curtis, David Simons, David Bill, Tom Fields, Ralph Johnson, Daniel Olmstead, Dave Wilson, Earl Brewer, Frank Casagni, Allen McIntosh, Andrew Geddes, Ron Clifford, Gary Cicognani, Porter Harvey Jr., Steve Jarvis, Rich Cianciolo, John Kelmelis, Gus Della Ghelfa, John Homgren, Jerry Ringstad, Michael DiPippo, Dave Iffland, and Anthony Giannattasio. There were also many sponsors, far too many to list, but a few of the now bygone business sponsors included: Haydon Manufacturing, LaPorta Ambulance, Katzman's Drug Store, Richard's Sport Store, Maiden Lane Cleaners, Boot Shop, North End Print Shop, Bolomey's Paint Store, Patten Jewelers, Geiger Brothers, Zanderigo's Gas Station, Morrison's Hardware, Torrington Creamery, Mar-Lyn Press, Tip-Top, Band Box, Dzialo's

Market, Doyle's Pharmacy, Susla Pharmancy, Neri's Gas Station, Dari-Delite, Brunswick Sport Products Company, Excelsior Laundry, Torrington Lumber Company, and Padelford's Atlantic Station (the gas station at the finish line on East Main).

(Above, a 1960 *Torrington Register* news clipping entitled "Preparing For Derby Day." Twelve-year-old Bill Russell is shown holding the steering wheel of his race car, which is under construction. The bulkheads can be seen, as well as the large brake pedal. The outer shell, the car's "skin" will be the last thing to be built. Other Derby-ists in the picture are, L-R: Frank Arigoni and Roger Waltos - race committee members, along with chief car inspector Addo Bonetti, and William Russell - Bill's father. They seem to be studying a rules booklet which, among other things, cites specific physical characteristics and dimensions that must be adhered to when constructing the "soap box.")

As was traditional, a parade kicked off Derby Day. The 1960 parade was led by Ronnie Clifford in a go-cart, followed by the Marine Corps Color Guard, a band from the Torrington Musicians Union, and Miss Torrington, Barbara Viarengo. Bill Russell won his first heat, as did Mike Boyle, Roger Richard, Cliff Curtis, et al. The finals pitted the 1959 runner-up Albert Gallo (sponsored by former state representative Jimmy Piscitelli) against John Kelmelis (sponsored by the Torrington Post Office Employees). In what was described as "a thrilling finish," the younger Albert Gallo won and followed his brother's lead to Akron, Ohio.

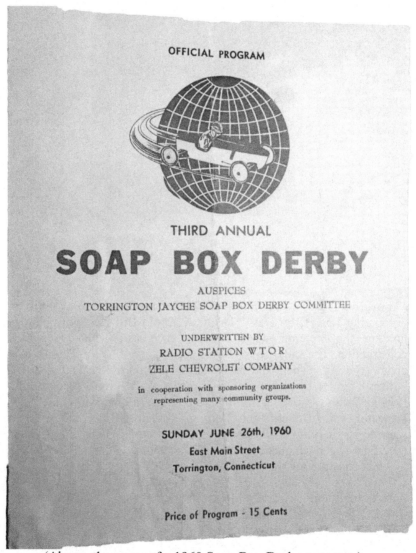

(Above, the cover of a 1960 Soap Box Derby program.)

(Above, an undated birdseye view of the finish line of the annual Soap Box Derby, circa 1958-'60. The racer in Lane 1 - far right - is 20 feet beyond the finish, while the racer in Lane 2 is 20 feet from the finish. The racer in Lane 3, on the far left is exactly *at* the finish line and is partly obstructed by the telephone pole. In the foreground stands White Way Laundry, followed by Globe Cleaners. Hillside Pharmacy is barely visible in the far right. This is where East Elm forks off.)

. . . The next year, 1961, and indeed for almost the next decade (1961-1970), if Torrington competitors wanted to race, they had to race out-of-town. In 1961 a group of 12 Torrington area boys competed at Veterans Memorial Park in East Hartford. They were Skip Day, Carl Muller, John Holmgren, Frank Casagni, Floyd Amicone, Lance Watts, John Kelmelis, Ronald Doucette, Richard Dagenais, Gerry Dagenais, Ron Clifford, and Don LaRocco. Five of these boys won their first heat. No one made it past the second round. WTOR did a remote broadcast of the event for perhaps the first *and* last time. Carl Muller won a prize for "Best Upholstery." Sidebar: The Torrington Historical Society has Carl Muller's soap box derby in its collection. . . In 1962, a busload of Torrington supporters traveled to Henderson Park in West Hartford to cheer on the local racers. Six Torrington entrants: Jerry Dagenais, Michael Fritch, Carl Muller, James Way, Skip Day, and Donald Marracino won their first two heats before losing. It was a very good showing. . . In 1963 Donald Marracino won three heats but lost in the finals of his Class A division to the eventual winner, Richard Rowley of South Glastonbury. A large number of Torrington supporters once again rooted on the boys. Other Torrington competitors that day who won their first 2 heats were Leonard "Skip" Day, Michael Rossi, David Bilak, Karl Ollesen, Stephen Dowling, William Burinskas, Mike Fritch, and Carl Muller. . . Judging by the past, it's a pretty safe bet to say that from 1964-'70, Torrington youths *did* race *somewhere* in Connecticut. There was just no reporting in the local press of who, when, or where, much less the outcomes. . . In 1971 the race returned to East Main. *The Torrington Register* reported that it was "the first running of the derby in several years." Major understatement. The Soap Box Derby had been gone absent from our local streets for a full 10 years, and as if discovering soulful sustenance after a prolonged famine/drought, thousands of Soap Box Derby fans once again lined "a sun-baked East Main." East Main itself was lined with used tires as a safety precaution. Al Eyre was the master of ceremonies, and the finals came down to David Echuk from Northfield, a finalist the previous year in Waterbury. And Tom Deering of Torrington. It was reported that Echuk's car "seemed to jump ahead with 18 feet to go," and he won by a foot. . . For the next 3 years, 1972-'74, the race moved to Kinney Street, a quiet Torrington roadway that parallels Route 8 and crosses the well known and highly used Winthrop Street. The race in those years was owned by the Monat brothers: Darryl, Danny, and

Dave, with a different brother winning in each of the 3 consecutive years.

(Above, looking down from near the top of Kinney Street on an early autumn day in 2019. The hill goes down, crosses Winthrop [which is barely visible as an indentation near the top] then starts back up. Note the 30 mph speed limit sign on the right. A typical soap box racer hits 20-30 mph. Happy Note: If anyone exceeded 30 mph during those early 1970's races, there's no record that the TPD ticketed them. . .)

On June 12, 1972, the festivities kicked off with The Vagabonds leading the entrants up the hill. Among the entrants were the first ever female contestants: Cheryl Wesolowski and Gail Coretto. Robert Christian was the race director, and approximately 1200 fans lined the race course. When the street dust settled, Darryl Monat, who was sponsored by Gerard's Photographers, was declared the winner. Richard Begey was second, Tim Mobob third. Sidebar: "Gerard's Photographers" was owned by Gerard Ringstad, who himself had been an early Torrington Derby contestant. . . As was usual, the June 1973 race followed a 4 month construction period which was overseen by the Torrington Jaycees. Forty contestants competed. Safety was always a #1 concern, and despite 2 cars smashing into the tires at the end of the track when their brakes failed *and* another going out-of-control near the finish line and hitting the used tire, side barrier, no injuries were reported. The '73 race was won by Danny Monat in a car sponsored by Competition Speed. It was one of the closest finishes ever. *The Torrington Register* reported, "Mary Smith gave the woman's libbers a lot to shout about before losing out in the final heat." Mary Smith was from East Hartford, and her car was a low-slung racer that rose slightly in the back. She tucked her head into that space, tilted it forward, and was completely aerodynamic. In the finals, though she

(Above, Mary Smith in 1973 spins her wheels to check balance and freedom of rotation.)

lost by a mere foot, perhaps less, the newspaper gushed, "She captured the heart of every feminist on hand." For winning the plunge down Kinney Street, 11-year-old Danny Monat took home a $500 U. S. Savings Bond and got to continue his racing at The Nationals in Akron, Ohio. Mary Smith won a trophy and a $200 Savings Bond. Added Bonus: A bonafide celebrity handed out the prizes. Spyder Lockhart, star defensive back for the New York Giants, looking sharp in a tie and plaid sports jacket, smiled for the photographers and posed with the racers. . . In 1974, it was clear that the magic had worn off soap box racing in Torrington. Only 15 contestants entered to include 3 girls, and only about 250 spectators showed up to watch the Kinney Street action. Probably to stretch out the proceedings and up the excitement factor, the Jaycees went with double elimination, i.e. a racer had to be defeated twice to be out. The race was in July and was covered by sportswriter and photographer John Torsiello. Positive Spin: The double elimination added value to a day for which the young participants had worked long and hard for. Again, a Monat won. Dave Monat, crouching low in a racer sponsored by Zele Chevrolet, beat Rob Kuhlburg of Winsted by a car length. Kuhlburg had finished 3rd the year before.

(Above an unidentified racer on the starting ramp on Kinney Street in 1974. The patriotic red-white-and-blue [the car's actual colors] paint job must have been an anomaly in a year in which the country was still being torn apart by The Vietnam War. Ironically it was the first year that the sponsor, Torrington Parkade Cinema, had come into existence, while it was the last year the race would be in existence. . . Photographer: Thomas Wootton. Photo: Collection of the Torrington Historical Society.)

Sadly, 1974 was the end of soap box racing in Torrington. The next year, 1975, only 5 youths showed interest in entering. The event needed a minimum of 18-20 to make it worthwhile. The Jaycees cited the added problem of rising costs. Thus, in 1975 the Torrington Soap Box Derby in Torrington folded. It hasn't been run since. . . I suppose sociologists might cite an ever complex world in which both youth and adults have more options at how to spend their leisure time, as a major factor for the demise of soap box racing in Torrington. But regardless of what finally did the race in, the years that it *did* run were a happy time in our valley. An innocent era of young boys and girls puzzling over construction diagrams, dreaming of defying gravity, of racing the wind. Of being crowned champion. And, for a glorious time those wheeled warriors gave themselves *and* our town something wonderful to cheer about. The stuff that boys' and girls' dreams are made of. . .

Responses included: "I remember Tom Zampini usually had a fast car. I think he won it a couple of times." . . . "Later on, they moved the Derby to the hill below the high school, and I drove one of Zeller Tire's trucks bringing the cars back to the top." . . . "I competed the first year. John Thomas helped me build the car, and I finished 2nd in my heat. We raced down East Main starting at New Harwinton Road. Tom Zampini won.". . . "I worked on one of the East Main races, for WTOR. Not sure which year, but probably 1959. Picked up a hellofa sunburn on my arms, as I recall." . . . "Yep, came straight down Kinney to East Elm Street. They blocked off Winthrop Street before the bridge, and people sat on the side of the road. One side was the grassy side of the highway, and the other was the sidewalks in front of apartments and the Overhead Door Company when it was located there. The Derby brought about 400 people from the area to include boy scouts and others. The Monat family was the family to beat. They lived on Garden Street. It was a great event." . . . "My best friend raced in it, not sure what year. We were both excited to hear it ran down Kinney Street because the daredevils in us thought it was Kennedy Drive." . . . "In 1971 it was on East Main Street and started by Doctor's McKenna's house and ended by Burger King. Father Joe Graziani was one of the judges." . . . "I remember the 1971 race. I lived 3 houses down from the start, on the block of New Harwinton Road, East Main, and Torrington Heights. I watched it from my front porch." . . . "I remember those days. I used to walk down to see the races in the 1960s." . . . "I remember sitting in front of Harry Hamzy's house to watch it." . . . "I competed in 1971 and was sponsored by Fitzgerald Manufacturing. It started on East Main and finished about where La Cucina is today. I also remember an older soap box derby car hanging in the rafters of the Dranginis family garage on New Harwinton Road in the sixties, i.e. a car from the earlier era races." . . . "I remember a soap box being put together in a cellar. It was blue, and Greg Prince eventually rode it. I'd say the year was 1971, and the race was from around McKennas down to Burger King." . . . "I'm not sure what year it was, but one of the Gallos won it, and I participated. It was the 1st time that I was ever in a police car, i.e. my soap box had been sponsored by the TPD and my car was painted black-and-white to resemble a police cruiser. LOL" . . . "I was in the Jaycees back in the earliest years of the Torrington Derby. We were assigned to one boy, and it was our job to assist him. We'd pop in every so often at his house, I forget how often, and answer any questions he had, and maybe make some recommendations. An important thing was to insure that the brake worked. It was a simple thing. A single board with a piece of rubber on it dropped to the ground. Applied pressure and friction did the rest. My kid nailed a chunk of rubber from an old tire to the board. It worked well. In the weeks before the race, we ran a test for all cars on one of those hills around Oak Avenue. It was a small hill. We ran a couple of cars at a time. If a car couldn't stop on that little hill, the brake would have to be redone and reinspected. There was only one major problem in those early years, one cheater. This kid's car was getting a tremendous 'jump' off the line. It'd shoot forward when the ramp went down, and he'd have a length-or-two lead before the cars had gone 30 feet. We finally inspected the car after one run, and it turned out that the father had rigged a spring-and-weight system in the nose. When the ramp went down, the kid would release the spring, the weight would shoot forward, and the car would charge into the lead. We DQed the young man. It's only too bad we couldn't have DQed the father too." . . . "I remember they drove the winner back up East Main in an open convertible, and the crowd cheered and went wild! Those races were a lot of fun. They *were* a big deal."

(Above, a postcard invitation to the 1959 post-race picnic. Who knew there were Derby "movies"! No doubt a good time was had by all.)

Post: THE Pond

Besse Pond. THE Pond. Whether or not you ever hung out there, played basketball on the outdoor court, ice skated on the frozen surface to the background music of Ritchie T, fished, or just passed it coming-and-going from school, it was, and *still* is, a gem on Winthrop Street.

(Left, Besse Pond in the spring of 2012. The basketball court is in the far background. The bronze plaque on the stone in the foreground reads: "ELLSE BESSE PARK. Given for the recreation of the youth of Torrington in memory of a devoted mother by her grateful son MAJOR WILLIAM EU-CENE BESSE. August 15, 1927. The hope of a city is in its youth."

Responses included: "Very many fond memories of going there as a kid." . . . "Loved Besse Pond. Have the best memories of ice skating there. The best part for me was those handsome boys who would pull my hat off. I thought I was so cool! Boys taking my hat! Do you think things have changed?" . . . "Haha. Nahhhh. Teens still play grabby gropey. Girls still love it and I believe initiate a lot of it. Somethings never change, though the skating is gone at Besse Pond. Hope you got your hat back." . . . "I have great memories of ice skating there as a 7th grader. I got to skate with a few attractive 8th grade beauties until they found out I was a 7th grader, then the gig was up." . . . "I remember ice skating there, and the DJ Richie Tee would play the music, the popular 45s of the day. He also DJed many of the YMCA dances." . . .

(Right, Richie Tee, a.k.a. Rich Tebecio in 1988. He sadly died in January 1994, but by then the platters had long stopped spinning at The Pond.)

"I remember ice skating, basketball, hitting rocks into the pond with sticks, but NO swimming ever. The city put up a seasonal sign in the North End that told of the status of the ice on Besse Pond, whether it was safe to skate or not. I always was thrilled when it went 'green', or whatever that signal was." . . . "I remember fishing there with a friend of mine, if you could call it that. We didn't catch a thing. I hadn't fished before that one time, and I haven't fished since. Besse Pond did me in." . . . "In recent years they've had some fishing outings/contests there, so I assume it's periodically stocked these days." . . . "I was a playground supervisor there in the summer. It was a good job except for the older kids who hung out there. They were a real pain in the ass." . . . "Guys used to go down there after school and settle heated differences. Back then it was done with fists."

(Left, some teens fooling around on Besse Pond in the winter of 1972. It's just possible that they're on a self proclaimed break from classes at nearby THS.)

(Above, a young solitary skater tries some moves on the Besse Pond ice during the winter of 1987. Torrington High School and a couple of older skaters can be seen in the background.)

. . . "I had my first date there!" . . . "I remember meeting a 7th grade girl there in the summer when I was a freshman. I tried making out with her, but she wasn't going for it. Besse Pond might have been a hot hangout, but she sure wasn't." . . . "I spent my entire youth there. Skating in the winter and playing hoops in the summer." . . . "I remember Lou The Cat playing basketball there. He sure could jump." . . . "I remember all the good times we spent at The Pond, both winter and summer with Janice and Roberta and the rest of the gang. Good memories!" . . . "In the 1920s when my father was a teenager he had a little stand there and sold hot dogs to skaters. I think - not completely sure - that my grandfather who died in the 1930s had an interest in the real estate there. I loved skating on that pond at night when I was in 7th grade. The music Richie Tee played is still with me: 'Walk Like A Man.' Paul and Paula. Skeeter Davis - 'Don't they know it's the end of the world.' 'It's my party and I'll cry if I want to.' 'My boyfriend's back and there's gonna be some trouble.' All pre-Beatle that winter, and I loved it." . . . "I don't think they could have picked a more beautiful setting for the high school. Well done!"

(Below, a corner of Besse Pond with T.H.S. in the background, circa 1963-'64 not long after the school opened. It truly *was* a beautiful setting.)

Post: The Genesis Of The T.H.S. "Red Raiders"

I was recently asked by a THS faculty member if I knew the evolution/history of the name "Red Raiders." This was asked in conjunction with a comment that a movement was in the early stages to do away with the "Indian" motif. This was my written response (sorry for the length). . . "Unfortunately I have never come across any explanation in writing how the "Red Raiders" got that name. I believe the original (or at least going back a loooooong way) school colors were red-and-white. I have a THS class ring from 1918 and the stone is red. I also have a pennant from 1914 and the colors are red-and-white. On a decal from the early 1940s, Torrington High was referred to as the "Big Red," but no mention of Raiders or Indians. They were also called the Red-and-White. And while there is nothing that I'm aware of in writing to explain the genesis of the phrase "Red Raiders," years ago Art Perret (THS Class of 1937, WWII paratrooper) told me that it was HE who first linked the name "Raider" to THS teams. Art Perret was a sports columnist for the Waterbury *Republican-American* back in the late 1940s/early 1950s. Why he called THS athletes "Raiders," I never asked. Wish that I had. Taking my best guess, I'd say it was because of the sharp "R" alliteration. Art Perret always did have style. The name caught on in the early 1950s, I think, around 1953-'54. . . Did it originally refer to Native Americans *or* John Brown's rebels? Best guess would be Indians, as the Indian motif in sports was pretty common for many bygone years/decades. . . Fully researching this would mean pouring over old X-Rays looking for references to "Raiders," reading the class histories in the yearbooks from that era, and for the truly dedicated going through the microfilm of *The Torrington Register*, perhaps even looking for Art Perret's columns in the Waterbury *Republican*. SIDEBAR: I know many schools have gotten rid of the "Indian" name and logo. The major league Cleveland Indians, with their Chief Wahoo, is perhaps the latest. And if the name offends, I'm all for changing it. However, I've never heard anyone complain about Torrington students/athletes being called Red Raiders. I'm also a lover of traditional and continuity, and as such will always be a Red Raider myself. Thought: Maybe the THS student body should have a debate on changing the name, and a vote if it even *should* be changed." . . . Personal History: When I got my first varsity letter in late winter 1963, athletes would get the logo of their sport on their Raider jacket with their name inside the logo. Swimmers such as myself got a fish. It was this way in the years before me too, but with one notable exception. When ordering a Raider jacket in the late 1950s - the early 1960s, a letter winner could get an "Indian" head instead of a football, winged foot, basketball, baseball, dolphin, etc. Some did. There were at least 2 variations. One was a majestic feathered "chief;" the other looked more like Chief Wahoo of the Cleveland Indians.

(Below left, Art Frigo in 1959 wears the "majestic featured chief" logo on his Raider jacket. On the right, in 1960, Bob Geiger wears the more light-spirited Chief Wahoo version.)

Whichever was chosen, it definitely cemented the phrase "Red Raider" to the image of a Native American. And we Red Raiders definitely saw that as a positive thing.

Responses included: "Thanks for the history lesson!" . . . "All I can say is GO RAIDERS." . . . "I totally agree with the concept of tradition. I've always believed that a school's/team's mascot was chosen as a symbol of a winning attitude and strength, quite the opposite of being any kind of negative racism." . . . "Strange, since we referred to our colors as maroon and white." . . . "A movement to change the name and image doesn't surprise me. Today's world looks at things differently than our world did in the 1960s." . . . "Too many people taking offense at just about everything!" . . . "I'm surprised that they haven't already changed the team name, or at least the Native American image that goes with it." . . . "I think that the Indian image should *not* be used. I hope it *does* change. I believe that some Native Americans are offended by being called 'red' and having their image used as a mascot. I know that we can be overly politically correct, but if someone is offended, we shouldn't continue to do what they find offensive." . . . "Are Irish people offended by the Notre Dame logo? The stereotypical, Irish cartoon leprechaun with fists up? I'm sure some are." . . . "Despite my Irish heritage, I am not one bit annoyed by the image used by the 'Fighting Irish!' " . . . "I am a 1960's Red Raider and take no offense to the Indian image. The warrior looks strong, and he's determined to be the best." . . . "When I went to Quinnipiac, the team name was the Braves. Now they are the Bobcats. Ugh! Perhaps there should be a counter movement to keep the Red Raider image." . . . "I like the big 'feathered' chief!" . . . "Keep the logo."

(Below, a THS maroon-and-white pennant, circa late 1960s.)

Some Miscellaneous Red Raider Images

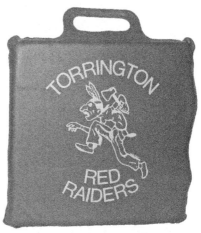

(Above, 2 seat cushions. The one on the left is from the 1960s, the one on the right from the mid-1970s. . . Below, a large THS blanket from the 1990s, with a bookcase backdrop.)

Post: Autumn Thoughts At Hillside Cemetery

Death - the final frontier. I came to peace years ago in Vietnam that one of these days I am going to die. Back then I distinctly thought it could be sooner, rather than later. And now here I am, 50 years later, still walking the earth, still reasonably healthy, still making plans for the future, though admittedly not so far in advance anymore. Time has collapsed, compacted itself, the end a helluva lot closer than the beginning. Still, it's not something I lose sleep over, and one of the reasons is Hillside Cemetery. I was there this morning, and looking over the little hollow, ablaze in autumn colors, where I'll be put to rest someday, I felt a sense of peace. I always do at Hillside. I know cemeteries exist to give comfort to the living, and the Walnut Street graveyard does that for me and I hope others. . . One final thing. Should any of you visit Hillside after I've passed, don't expect to make contact with me. I have absolutely NO plans to hang out in a cemetery, though it IS comforting now. Peace, and enjoy this great autumn weather.

Responses included: "Quick story: My father is buried in a great old cemetery in the center of New Milford. Many years ago, I visited the grave alone, on a very overcast day. I scooched down and while chatting with him, I used my keys to remove a bit of lichen from the engraving. I finished, said to him, 'Well that looks better,' and just then, a tiny hole opened in the cloud overhead. Spotlight on my Dad and me. Only us! Treasured memory for sure." . . . "I hope to be able to read more of your thought provoking posts in the years to come." . . . "By far, the best and most beautiful cemetery! I know exactly where you are. My cousin is buried in that area." . . . "I miss walking there. But I'll be there one day myself! And my stone is there too!" . . . "Hillside is beautiful. Visit it about three times a week. We have four graves that we take care of. I love to water the flowers early in the morning in the summer. Very peaceful. Besides, nobody gives me grief if I'm late, and I like the option to leave in my car, instead of the big black car leaving without me." . . . "I like to walk through old cemeteries and read the stones. Lots of history there." . . . "Well said. I have family there, and it always looks beautiful." . . . "I have to admit, I saw the picture of the cemetery, and I knew I was going to like your post for the simple fact that I knew you'd spell 'cemetery' correctly." . . . "My mom, dad, and step-father are all buried there along with my paternal grandparents. I have a plot there, although I don't believe I will be using it. I used to walk the perimeter for exercise." . . . "This is so beautifully written. Vietnam did terrible things to all those young men, my husband included. Peace is what hopefully we can all achieve. Thank you." . . . "You should give lectures on the subject. I felt much better about my mortality after reading this. Well done!" . . . "One of the best cemeteries around. My parents are buried there along with other relatives. When I'm back in town to visit graves, it is a great place to reflect." . . . "Hillside Cemetery is where I always walked my dog when I had one. So beautiful." . . . "Played there with my pals in the 1950s, never got tired of the place. With permission, camped out in the woods behind with my scout patrol. Parents are there now (not camping!)." . . . "It makes me happy that our parents are buried there, right down the hill from where they built our house." . . . "You are pulling at my heart strings here. My wife's parents and her grandparents are buried there. Also buried there is a `little baby girl from our family who died at birth. Your words are touching and right on point. Thanks for your thoughts. I'll be attending my Torrington High School reunion this weekend, and Hillside will be one of my stops!" . . . "Torrington has quite a few cemeteries: new St. Francis, old St. Francis, St. Peter's, Center Cemetery, Sons of Jacob, West Torrington Cemetery (Goshen Road) - but Hillside is *the* best."

Epilogue

And thus we come to the end of the 8th "Torrington" book. Confession: When I sat down to write this one, I thought I'd be mainly *editing* the original Facebook posts, but it didn't take long for me to realize that my expectations were way off. That there was going to have to be a *lot* more 2019 research and original writing for this to be even close to the quality book I intended. Thus many of the original posts became longer and more fact-filled in the process. And all comments were edited for grammar and to insure anonymity.

As I searched out the old posts for interesting material, I discovered that many of the posts on Facebook, while interesting in their narrow context, did not lend themselves well to book content. For example, I had posted over 100 pictures of my own 1966 THS class to include many newspaper clippings. But such a narrow focus on one class did not translate well into the kind of topical material that the average reader would be interested in. Great for THS Facebook, not so wonderful for mass appeal. Ultimately I found myself researching original subjects, such as Torrington barbers and Torrington fires, because I felt that they were subjects that would have not only great Facebook appeal, but also much broader Torrington interest. I hope they did.

While I *did* include many of my original THS and Torrington posts here, many more were excluded. Length was a concern, as was appropriateness. For example, one of my Facebook photo albums involved around 35 pictures of vintage Torrington calendars. Members of my THS Facebook page commented on each one and on the businesses they represented. While it was an interesting historical post and response section, it simply did not translate into a good fit for a book. To be effective, I would have had to pretty much devote a full page to each calendar, i.e. 35 pages. It was just too much visual, for too little content. Sidebar: Maybe someday I'll do a book on *just* my hoards of Torrington memorabilia.

If you've enjoyed this book and think now that you'd like to join my THS Facebook page, there are only a few requirements. Be sure you're a THS graduate from roughly the years from 1972 or earlier. AND, be sure to answer all 3 questions when you request to join. *Very* important. . . A special closing thanks to the staff at the Torrington Historical Society: Mark, Gail, and Carol. In addition to competently steering me to the correct sections of the Society's archives, they also gave me permission to use some *very* key photos

from their collection. Much thanks for your gracious generosity.
Eternally grateful.

Peace and prosperity to all.
Happy Torrington Days.
Go Raiders!
Paul Bentley
Autumn 2019

Made in the USA
Monee, IL
12 December 2020